Agendas and Decisions

AGENDAS AND DECISIONS

How State Government Executives
and Middle Managers Make
and Administer Policy

DOROTHY F. OLSHFSKI
and
ROBERT B. CUNNINGHAM

STATE UNIVERSITY OF NEW YORK PRESS

Published by
State University of New York Press, Albany

For information, contact State University of New York Press, Albany, NY
www.sunypress.edu

Production by Marilyn P. Semerad
Marketing by Anne M. Valentine

Library of Congress Cataloging-in-Publication Data

Olshfski, Dorothy F.
  Agendas and decisions : how state government executives and middle managers make and administer policy / Dorothy Olshfski, Robert B. Cunningham.
     p. cm.
  Includes bibliographical references and index.
  ISBN 978-0-7914-7323-8 (hardcover : alk. paper)
  ISBN 978-0-7914-7324-5 (pbk. : alk. paper)
    1. State governments—United States—States—Management. 2. Administrative agencies—United States—States—Management. 3. Executive departments—United States—States—Management. I. Cunningham, Robert, 1937– II. Title.

JK2446.5.O48 2008
352.3'30973—dc22

                                                                2007013151

10 9 8 7 6 5 4 3 2 1

Contents

Preface

Practice expertise is the knowledge of how to do things, executing competent performance; theory expertise is verbalizing, generalizing about what we know (Sandelands 1990, 235). These domains are rarely conjoined. Donald Polkinghorne (1988) wrote *Narrative Knowing and the Human Sciences* because of "an unresolved personal conflict between my work as an academic researcher on the one hand and as a practicing psychotherapist on the other. . . . I have not found the findings of academic research of much help in my work as a clinician" (p. ix).

Like Polkinghorne and Sandelands, we seek to connect practice knowledge and theory knowledge about how state-level public executives and managers decide and implement policy. We have studied a management system where the governor believes in and practices the principles espoused by leadership theorists:

1. focus on one or two important substantive problems or initiatives
2. work with stakeholders to protect the organization and to obtain the resources necessary to address those problems or initiatives
3. hire good people and authorize them to act

Lamar Alexander, governor of Tennessee from 1979 to 1987, sent cabinet members to the Kennedy School, where they were drilled in these practices. His commissioner of personnel established the Tennessee Government Executive Institute (TGEI) to provide an analogous three-week program each summer for mid-level state managers.

We managed the program component of TGEI during its first five years. We attended every session for most of those years, and commencing in year two interviewed program participants, asking each to tell stories of their decisions.

In the casual conversations that permeate such off-site, residential program environments, we learned "from the inside" about governance. Our mid-level contacts in the various state agencies facilitated research access to the commissioners considered the "top ten" during Alexander's tenure as governor.

Based upon stories from interviews with middle managers and cabinet members, and framed by a decision model, we test management decision-making theories and propose hypotheses. Scholars can assess the utility of the hypotheses for theory knowledge; practitioners can extend their skill repertoire as they "watch" competent managers at work through the stories and then reflect on the stories. The reader interested in the persons or historical period or location can gain insight from the inside on governance during the Alexander years.

We hope that readers will not only learn from but also enjoy this story and that both practice knowledge and theory knowledge can emerge.

Acknowledgments

George Bass was director of training when the Tennessee Government Executive Institute (TGEI) began in 1983. The high regard with which he was held throughout state government for his personal character and professional competence attracted able middle managers to TGEI during its early years. George directed TGEI, the authors designed and managed the program. George navigated the white water of Tennessee state government for us, and we are grateful.

Participants in TGEI during its first ten years schooled us in the ways of middle management in state government by their stories, anecdotes, activities, and interrelationships. TGEI managers work hard, play gently, and have a sense of humor. If these people represent Tennessee middle managers, as we think they do, and if they resemble state managers throughout the United States, which we hope, then decisions devolved to state middle managers will be as competently, carefully, and conscientiously handled as a governance system will allow.

Over the years, graduate assistants in the Graduate School of Public Administration at Rutgers-Newark and in the Political Science Department at UT-Knoxville have helped with this project. We have appreciated the opportunity to work with them and are grateful for their assistance. Thanks to Sydney Olshfski for the original cover design concept, later adapted and executed by freelance artist Ken Schrider.

Our families have been a source of loving support throughout the many years we worked on this project: Gary, Seth, Sydney, Paul, Milli, Nina, Ann, Bailey, Rachel, and Robert.

Thank you all.

ONE

Introduction

AGENDAS AND DECISIONS is about state government leadership and management. The executive branch of state government does more than administer the laws of the state; the executive branch creates policy that impacts people's lives. Making policy and implementing policy are the everyday tasks of cabinet members and middle managers in state government. The administrator decision process resembles the legislator decision process, that is, hierarchy matters, structure matters, culture matters, experience matters, background and personality matter (Bosso 1994). Cabinet members and middle managers in the executive branch must deal with these constraints, and they must implement as well as decide. Using a simple decision model to frame managers' and executives' stories about situations they faced, this book describes, analyzes, and explains how middle managers and cabinet members made and carried out decisions during the Tennessee governorship of Lamar Alexander.

With the erosion of citizen trust in the national government, and with decisions by the Supreme Court strengthening the role of states, state governments have both the authority and the favor of citizens as they address the state's problems (Jennings 1998). For governors seeking to be seen as "strong," the management structure and practices followed by Lamar Alexander, governor from 1979 to 1987, provide a useful exemplar. During his eight years in office Alexander took initiative while enhancing the power and decision latitude of the executive. His public opinion ratings were exceptional; state managers were satisfied in their jobs; and outside experts praised Alexander's performance.[1]

A state governor's years in office are not automatically smooth or successful. In 2003, Gray Davis of California, having committed no malfeasance of office, was recalled and replaced by Arnold Schwarzenegger. Don Sundquist, Tennessee's governor from 1995 to 2003, in his second term

1

endured acrimonious criticism from legislators and the public, and most Tennesseans were relieved when his term ended. Davis (a Democrat) and Sundquist (a Republican) were decent people, able politicians with long careers in public service, but they could not establish and sustain credible state-level leadership and management systems. Alexander was successful, and his management practices contributed to his success.

Alexander developed an effective working relationship with the legislature. A well-organized lobbying effort helped the governor pass his primary legislative initiative, education reform. Incremental tax increases paid for new programs. We believe that the foundational components of the Alexander administration were his leadership style and management system: communicating on a regular basis directly with citizens and delegating responsibility to the cabinet for all decisions other than the governor's primary legislative initiatives. Devolving responsibility represents an effective governance model. Governors Matheson of Utah (Cox 1991; Matheson 1986), Sargeant of Massachusetts (Weinberg 1976), and Lucy of Wisconsin (Adamany 1989) are reported to have adopted this style, but detailed descriptions of their management systems and impact on the state's managers have not been reported.

Many governors manage another way; they maintain a highly controlled management system, with little independent decision authority granted to their cabinet appointees. Desiring to establish a reputation for effectiveness and probity, control-oriented governors may worry that a cabinet member might embark on a personal agenda, or that some seemingly inconsequential remark or incident emanating from an agency could be seized upon by rivals hoping to gain political advantage. By centralizing authority in the governor's office and minimizing the decision latitude granted to cabinet members, costs, errors, and the risk of scandal are presumably reduced. In that control model, the governor and the appointed staff initiate policy changes, both legislative proposals requiring substantial negotiation between the executive and legislative branches and minor administrative changes that can be implemented unilaterally by the agency. The relevant cabinet member may be ignored by the governor on policy initiatives affecting the agency. In a centralized, control-mode governance system, the cabinet member has a large implementation role, but a limited policy-making role. Tight, centralized control was not Alexander's system.

Theorists of leadership and management have reached consensus that for organization effectiveness, decision making should be pushed to the lowest feasible level. The chief executive officer must take responsibility for the overall direction of the organization, deal with the external environment to protect the organization, secure resources to support executive initiatives, and motivate middle managers and frontline employees. Governor Lamar Alexander preached and practiced these principles. He gave his managers books on management, brought in management experts to conduct training sessions, and sent his managers to management seminars. For Alexander, good policy and good governance emerged from good management.

In Alexander's devolved management system, the governor restricted his policy attention. On his primary initiative—education—the governor worked personally with staff, outside advisors, and Department of Education managers in crafting legislation and lobbying for its passage. The commissioner of education functioned as a middle manager, lobbying for and implementing the decisions made by a task force appointed by the governor. The other cabinet members had freedom of action regarding policy initiatives, subject to three constraints: (1) staying within budget, (2) avoiding negative press coverage, and (3) abstaining from actions that would instigate conflict between agencies. Alexander recruited some outstanding cabinet members and gave all cabinet members, except education, free rein. The governor's staff did not intrude into the agency's business unless one of the three constraints was violated, or unless the cabinet member requested assistance.

This book focuses not on Alexander the person but on executive and middle manager behaviors in Alexander's management system, specifically, decision and implementation actions at cabinet and subcabinet levels. Alexander subscribed to the simple advice for managers regularly articulated by mainstream scholars and management gurus for the past fifty years:

Hire good people.
Give them authority to make decisions.
Get them the resources they need.
Leave them alone.
Support and protect them.
If they make too many mistakes, remove them.

This is not the only effective management system, but it was effective for Alexander in Tennessee during his time as governor, and it constitutes a leadership/management model for a governor to consider.[2]

We viewed the operation of Alexander's management model from the inside, through the eyes of executives, middle-level managers, staffers, and close observers of the executive system. Cabinet members and middle managers tell of decisions they made and implemented, thereby offering pictures of state government in action. From their stories and from external evidence emerges a system of effective governance, and from that picture we test and propose theories of administrative decision making and implementation.

Tennessee government under Alexander was a high performing system (HPS). Peter Vaill (1998, 62) describes this research approach:

The number of social scientists who are trying to understand excellence in human systems is very small. Pathology is more accessible, and, for some, more fun. The question of what it takes to govern and lead a high performing system, and the question of how we are going to develop more men and women who are equipped to do so await the increased attention that I believe HPSs deserve.

Peter Drucker (2004) argues that an organization's best managers should be assigned to "opportunities," not "problems." Drucker's directive is supportive of "appreciative inquiry," (Srivastva and Cooperrider et al. 1990), and it matches our orientation to the interviews and writing. Appreciative inquiry (AI) does not focus on "problems" and "conflicts." Instead, it draws attention to areas of common understanding and builds on these areas of agreement to develop mutual trust and action plans. The competent managers with whom we conversed practiced appreciative management, although neither they nor we had heard of the concept at the time of our interviews. Alexander's cabinet members held in high regard the performance of state employees. Quoting Commissioner Simons, "State employees are really treasures if you treat them properly; they value their jobs and they work hard, but they need to be nurtured." This positive attitude of commissioners toward their subordinates pervaded each interview. Middle managers, given praise, responded with the exceptional performance that motivation theory expects.

One objective of this book is to build theory, to illustrate and explain a state government system that invests substantial power, authority, and responsibility with the cabinet rather than with the governor's staff. The usual image of bureaucratic decision making is the rational model, with power located at the apex of the organization. We began this study with the rational decision-making model as our framework, with incrementalism as an option that could emerge from the inquiry process. We found that the managerial decision process lacks clarity and precision. In the upper reaches of Alexander's governance system, neither hierarchy and the rational decision model nor incrementalism dominated. Agenda setting is a key component determining the problem definition and decision outcome (Barry et al. 1997; Baumgartner and Jones 1993; Kingdon 1984), and implementation is not always relegated to the middle levels or front line. *Agendas and Decisions* offers ideas on how executives use evaluation, and introduces the concept of density to explain the speed (or lack thereof) for administrative decision making.

Another objective of this book is to link theory and practice in a way that is helpful for those who wish to improve their management skills, and to understand why the attitudes and behaviors associated with those skills are important. We theorize about practice through stories. *Storytelling* as a data source was unusual back in the 1980s, but over the past two decades, accompanying the rise of postmodernism, stories have bloomed as evidence to communicate meaning (Hummel 1991; King and Zanetti 2005). Multiple interpretations are inherent in stories. The heart of postmodernism is that the reader is in charge (Rosenau 1992). No longer is the primary task to understand the author's or speaker's intent; rather, the axial point is the reader's or listener's interpretation. Orthodoxy is out; heterodoxy is in; and meaning emerges in and from the mind and heart of the hearer. Stories are the primary data source for this study.

The fall of the positivist monolith has brought forth a range of ideas and approaches for studying organizations. Berger's and Luckmann's (1967) *The Social Construction of Reality*, which argues for a subjectivist approach to understanding, and the writings of Karl Weick, especially his book *Sensemaking in Organizations* (1995), offer useful perspectives for understanding and explaining a manager's thinking processes. Barbara Czarniawska (1999) proposes *narrative as theory*. In *Writing Management* she maintains that a story contains theory, making the argument that Chester Barnard (1968), in his classic *Functions of the Executive*, arrived at his theories through intuition-based speculation. Practitioners are not aware of the theories they are applying (Czarniawska 1999). The aim of practice is action, not reflection. *Agendas and Decisions* connects reflection to action by theorizing practice through stories.

Chapter 2 describes the decision-making process model of identifying the problem, assessing alternative ways to solve the problem, solving it, implementing the solution, and assessing the effectiveness of the solution. A few of the stories told by managers touched on each step of the model. More usually, the model did not adequately explain the decision process in the stories of the executives and middle managers we interviewed.

Chapters 3–6 analyze the stories according to the stages of the decision model. Chapter 3 describes problem identification. Problems reach the manager's agenda by one of three portals: position, politics, or perspective. First, the problem can be within one's *position* description. It is a solid waste problem, and you are the director of solid waste. Or, you are responsible for antiquities, and an Indian burial site is found within a highway right-of-way. The problem comes directly to you. Second, *politics* pushes a problem onto your desk. People complain to the governor that they face long lines getting their drivers' licenses, and the problem is routed from the governor's office to the commissioner of safety; or the governor promises to reduce duplication in various kinds of inspections, and you are charged with inspecting the state's grocery stores or restaurants. Third, "*perspective*" is an important aspect of problem identification underappreciated in the administrative literature. Perspective impacts the problem-identification phase by framing a situation based upon the manager's vision or idea for something that needs to be done. This aspect of problem identification, called "agenda setting" in the policy-making literature, has not received much attention in the administrative arena.

Problems identified must be resolved, and chapter 4 presents ways managers assess alternative solutions to the issues they choose or are forced to face. In low-density situations the process can be straightforward and transparent.

The manager may check with colleagues, peers in other states, or a professional association for suggestions. The manager explores options, selects the best available one, clears the solution with a superior if necessary, and acts. If there is disagreement or the manager lacks the power to act unilaterally, then the issue languishes or goes to a higher level for decision.

High-density issues or environments demand meetings. The composition of the attendees may change from one meeting to the next. Issues thought resolved are reopened based upon new participants or fresh information. Problem definition and preferred solution change over time until an alignment of stakeholders coalesces around a solution. That window of opportunity may close, requiring that the issue loop back through the decision process. In a dense environment, solutions are never secure until implementation has been completed.

Politics takes different guises according to managerial level. Cabinet members worry about party politics; they are concerned that an issue for which they are responsible may escalate and explode in the media, divide Republicans from Democrats, damage their ability to manage effectively, and impact the governor. Middle managers, on the other hand, if they face politics coming from outside their agency, it is a politics of interest groups—some groups seeking benefits or advantages over other groups. Political parties or political personalities do not instigate the conflicts that face middle managers. From what we could see, partisan political decisions play out at the cabinet and governor levels, not down in the middle of the bureaucracy. Executive activities differ from middle manager activities.

Some managerial studies have shown that in defining and solving problems, executive roles and behaviors differ from middle manager roles and behaviors (Johnson and Frohman 1989; Kraut et al. 1989). Differences between executives and middles show clearly in our study. In problem identification, middles have less opportunity to select the problems on which they work. In making decisions, middle managers more often than executives are caught in a web of relationships requiring acquiescence from peers before a decision can be made. Executives, based upon the power of position, have a wider range of tools, options, and choices as they decide which issues to address, the strategies for addressing them, and actions to be taken.

Chapter 5 describes executive and middle manager involvement at the implementation stage. Implementation is the principal job of middle managers. Middle managers administer policy, often spending endless hours in meetings attempting to persuade those assembled to reach a decision on implementing a policy. Implementation is their primary usual responsibility. Executives, on the other hand, are described as setting the agency's agenda, acquiring the resources to accomplish the agency's tasks, and organizing the workload for the entire unit (Glenn 1985; Kraut et al. 1989). However, commissioner tenure is short, so to make an impact, to have their policy preferences implemented by the bureaucracy, several executives involved themselves directly in implementation. Some executive implementation stories are presented, and the implications are discussed.

Chapter 6 examines evaluation. Executives and middle managers looked at evaluation differently. Middle managers have learned to cover themselves: for the policies they discussed, they generally offered hard data to substantiate their successes. Executives, on the other hand, less often cited hard evidence. Executives appeared oblivious to failure. They did not fail. We discuss this contradiction between analysis and leadership.

To summarize, *Agendas and Decisions* combines the approach of Mintzberg (1973), who asked how managers do their jobs, with the writings of consultants such as Max DePree (1992), Peters and Waterman (1982), or Robert Quinn (1988, 1996), who offer practical guidance on how to be a leader and manager. The findings reported here both support previous research on differences among management levels and suggest corollaries to theories present in the general management literature but absent from previous research on state governance. Chapter 2 covers the decision model that frames the study; it then introduces the cultural environment and the density concept. Chapters 3–6 analyze the stories within the framework of the decision process model: identifying the problem, analyzing the situation and deciding what to do, implementing, and evaluating. Chapter 7, the conclusion, summarizes the main ideas. The Appendix describes our methodological journey from positivism to a qualitative approach. We begin with the decision process model, which includes the cultural environment and the concept of density.

TWO

The Decision Process Model, the Cultural Environment, and Density

A DECISION-MAKING MODEL offers a process for making decisions. A useful model is sufficiently broad to provide guidance on a wide range of decision-making situations, while having enough specificity to apply easily to the unique case at hand. Our four-stage model—defining the problem, assessing alternative solutions and choosing one, implementing the solution, and then evaluating the outcome (Denhardt et al. 2002, 126–29; Anderson 2006)—seeks to be useful for both the manager who uses the decision process, as well as for the student who wishes to understand it (see Figure 2.1).[1] The manager, alone or collaboratively, studies the situation, defines the problem, considers alternatives and consequences and chooses a solution, and then selects among implementation strategies to achieve the solution. Discussion may loop back to a prior stage from any point in the process. After implementation, the outcome may be evaluated.

"Decision environment" serves as an unconscious filter that assesses the acceptability for each alternative considered at each step of the process. "Density" influences the speed with which the issue can be resolved. The decision process model is a frame for thinking about and acting on decisions to be made; "decision environment" and "density" are concepts employed to help explain the actions of state-level executives and middle managers. This chapter will present the decision process model that framed our data collection, discuss the strengths and limits of that model, and then introduce the concept of "density," an aspect of the decision environment that we found crucial for understanding the amount of time it takes for an issue to traverse the decision process.

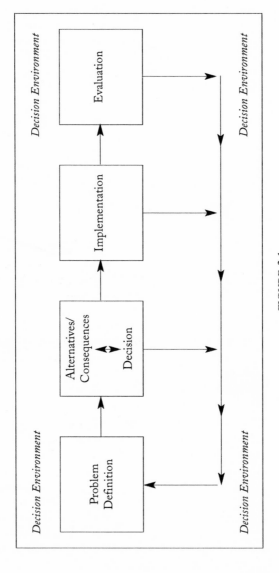

FIGURE 2.1
The Decision Process Model

DECISION PROCESS MODEL

A model or theory involves *knowing that*; practice involves *knowing how* (Sandelands 1990). A public administrator must be a planner (knowing that) *and* a doer (knowing how). The administrator anticipates and prepares based upon the theory presumed to underlie the situation, continuously adjusting as the plan is implemented, just as a baseball manager has to make decisions prior to each pitch while constantly readjusting contingency plans according to the play on the field. One does not just plan or just act; one plans and acts, simultaneously and continuously.

Barry et al. (1997) found that most of the managers they interviewed were not aware of their agenda processes; theory is present but employed unconsciously. A situation may emphasize any of three decision components: identifying the problem, deciding on a solution to the problem, or implementing the solution. One decision stage may be more important than another due to the nature of the situation or the perspective of the manager.

Problem Identification

"Problem" and "opportunity" are generally considered antonyms. Budget preparation in the face of declining revenues will normally be seen as a problem, or if revenues are increasing it will be seen as an opportunity. A creative manager may view things in exactly the reverse way, looking for opportunities to restructure as revenues decline, and planning for possible hard times ahead as revenues rise. Budget increases heighten the pressure on administrators to spend money on a politician's pet projects and can force the agency to undertake costly new projects to satisfy significant stakeholders. Middle managers in the Department of Conservation may view an increased capital budget with mixed emotions. Capital projects pushed by politicians can skew the agency's priorities as in subsequent years' maintenance costs for those projects bite into the agency's operating budget, threatening the organization's ability to maintain the quality of its ongoing programs. How the situation is defined impacts mightily on the solution selected. Thoughtful managers turn problems into opportunities. Some managers' stories emphasized the problem identification stage of the decision.

Emphasizing problem identification occurred when Finance and Administration (F&A) Commissioner Donelson defined a higher education problem/opportunity as insufficiently rigorous standards at the University of Tennessee. He received agreement from both the University of Tennessee-Knoxville and Governor Alexander to reduce enrollments in exchange for increased financial support from the state, an action the university supported enthusiastically. There was no significant decision-making stage, nor any implementation obstacles. Gaining agreement by the governor on the problem definition was the only problematic stage of the process.

Facing a difficult sexual harassment situation within the Department of Human Services, Commissioner Puett spent nearly a month attempting to define the problem. Once she combined appropriate social work practice with a consensus regarding the facts of the case, she was able to define the problem to her satisfaction, and the decision and implementation stages went quickly.

Inadequate attention to the problem definition stage of the process can lead to error. Commissioner Donelson identified the computer needs of the state as a centralized system controlled by the information division of his department. In our interview he admitted that he had incorrectly identified the problem. He belatedly came to understand the problem as overly centralized information systems that slowed line agency decision processes. The source of the wrong policy lay in a wrong problem definition.

Analyzing Alternatives and Making A Decision

Having defined the problem, what should the manager do? The model calls for exploring options, speculating on likely outcomes and calculating those probabilities, and then selecting a course of action. Stories told by the managers and executives rarely separated analysis of alternatives from making the decision. Seeking options, analyzing alternatives, and deciding what to do were intertwined. This finding challenges the accuracy of the model in depicting how managers go about making decisions.

In some stories, analyzing the alternatives and coming to a decision was the major focus. For example, the problem of too many civil service classification categories was unanimously agreed upon, but no agency wanted to constrain its flexibility by reducing its number of classification categories. Like military base closings at the federal level (base closings are desirable and important as long as the base being closed lies in someone else's congressional district), everyone readily agrees to reduce another's classification categories. Commissioner Akins in personnel had to convince both line workers and senior officials in each agency that employees would not be disadvantaged by reducing the number of civil service classes. Reducing as many classification categories as possible while maintaining sufficient legislative support to keep the proposal alive required a sensitive political touch by the commissioner at the decision stage. The commissioner and his managers working on the plan bounced around various alternatives and consequences as they sought a good plan acceptable to stakeholders. Formulating the plan was a time-consuming challenge, and once consensus was achieved on the proposal among the legislative leadership, success was assured. The final result looked as though it were a broad comprehensive plan, while in fact it was composed of a series of smaller decisions about alternatives that took place over time and involved many participants along the way. After the decision was made, implementation was tedious and time-consuming, but not problematic politically or administratively.

Selecting an Implementation Strategy

Implementation is the normal, expected work of middle managers; they take the articulated policy from those higher in the system and develop the routines for frontline employees to carry it out. It is not surprising that many of the middle managers' stories discussed an implementation strategy.

Implementation discussions also were present in executive stories. Executives are not seen as active participants in the implementation process; the literature on top executives has them identifying problems and deciding what to do. However, we found that executives' stories included substantial attention to implementation. In some cases, the commissioner was actively involved in the implementation. The implementation stage challenged Commissioner Simons, who was determined to change her agency's culture from control to service.

> I came in with the thought that this was a control agency that had no right to be a control agency, it was a service agency and that's the way it would be the most effective in state government.

> Q. How did you begin to sell that within your own department, how did you communicate [implement] the change?

> It is a hard thing to do, and I think that because we are comfortable with it now, that I am not doing justice to how uncomfortable I did feel in doing that in the beginning. I did feel uncomfortable. You can't help but feel a little silly talking about "great service" every time you get up, but I forced myself to do that, and even though assistant commissioners would have to appear with me at all these various functions, they would hear it over and over again. I have gotten to the point now where it just doesn't bother me at all. I continue to harp on great service, but the thing that has been very rewarding is that now they [middle managers in the agency] do too, and they have been doing it for quite some time.

Defining the problem took no time; deciding on a solution was implicit in the problem definition. Implementation was challenging and time-consuming. Altering the attitudes and behaviors of her employees required continuous attention to the message, including both rewards and punishments. She traveled to the various General Services Department offices throughout the state to communicate the goal.

Implementation stories by middle managers describe typical middle manager behaviors. In the process of implementing the decision made elsewhere the middle managers would identify the problems that would complicate implementation, find alternative ways to cope with those problems, decide how to proceed, and then act or disseminate a system of procedures.

Because often middle managers do not have effective control over those who must carry out the task, implementing requires skills in negotiation and communication in order to gain cooperation from others in the process.

Evaluation

Our decision model includes evaluation as the final component. Pressman and Wildavsky (1984) recommend that the principal guidelines of the evaluation stage be stated in advance, and that sufficient flexibility should be incorporated so that unexpected effects—both positive and negative—can be considered. We doubt that happened among our managers. Evaluation seems to be ongoing, almost a subconscious activity. Evaluation was not routinely mentioned, perhaps because the story was defined in advance as a success.

Middle managers and executives differed in how they viewed the evaluation process. Middle managers usually produced numbers to demonstrate success and talked of implementation as a group effort. Executives, on the other hand, used nonquantitative evidence to illustrate their success, although they sometimes would produce numbers when queried. Executives used the word "I" frequently when talking of evaluation, which seems to be related to their leadership role. Followership can be encouraged by creating an aura of success. Successful programs mean competent leaders, and the executives would communicate their program accomplishments to facilitate support for their other initiatives.

The Decision Process: Summary

We found that the decision-making process did not conform to a rigidly sequenced pattern. The decision process loops along; ideas are bounced back and forth, shunted off as they are deemed unworkable, incorporated if they generate enough support, or challenged until they are modified sufficiently to mollify stakeholders. The most troublesome stage in the decision process will vary. The primary obstacle may arise in defining the issue, or in resolving the issue, or at the implementation stage. All aspects of the decision are open to change when a policy encounters a technical, political, or cultural roadblock. General observations of the decision process are as follows:

1. Managerial situations involve "messy" issues (Parkhe 1993), "wicked" problems (Gortner 1991), which do not have a single correct definition or answer.
2. These situations encourage competing definitions, and managers see various problems or opportunities in a situation.
3. Being stymied or changing the answer at one stage of the process has implications for other stages of the process, causing a looping effect as the decision makers move back and forth among stages seeking a solution that satisfies the constraints at each stage.

In our interviews, when a respondent seemed to omit a decision stage, we would probe. This led to the discovery that managers did not view the overall process as we anticipated: they did not see distinct stages, and they did not follow a common pattern in addressing problems. The stories emphasized various stages of the decision process, and few decisions went smoothly through the steps in the model. The decision model, although not a metric followed by the managers and executives, serves to organize the chapter sequence for this book, because the stages of the model are useful categories for explaining how a decision is made.

Traditional science assumes that reality is objective and identical for every competent observer. The social constructionist approach to knowledge (Berger and Luckmann 1967) assumes that the manager creates reality from what is perceived. Each manager has a personal "mental map" (Miles and Huberman 1984, 131–32) that organizes the reality, and a personal definition of reality from their perspective—influenced by their personal job definition, agency priorities, constraints, and opportunities, or by their personal background and experiences.

Two people holding identical managerial positions may view agency priorities differently. The shape, direction, and activities of an agency could shift dramatically with a change of commissioner, with no apparent issue or problem forcing a change. Under a devolved administration such as Lamar Alexander's (who encouraged each commissioner personally to seek out and address the agency's needs), the commissioner's mental map had a strong impact on problem definition. Executives looked at the situation they faced and constructed a problem they thought they could solve. If it appeared their first problem definition was not able to be implemented the situation was reconstructed, and reconstructed again, until an achievable solution was found.

The decision maps found in the minds of the managers incorporate the components of the decision model used here, but the sequencing and linearity of the rational model were not validated. Each manager constructs a situation uniquely and moves among the components of the decision-making model until comfortable with the decision.

THE DECISION ENVIRONMENT

Managers do not make decisions in a vacuum. From becoming aware of a situation to evaluation, the decision-making process takes place in the context of a decision environment that includes cultural factors, organizational factors, and politics and issues.

Cultural Factors

A decision rarely strays far from the norms present in the environment. The culture does not readily acquiesce to change efforts by executives and middle managers. Culture resists innovation. Tennesseans sometimes refer to their state as "the buckle of the Bible belt," with the public holding a traditional suspicion of government and an aversion to government-initiated change. Each manager's story takes place against this cultural backdrop, and accommodating the culture in ways that do not impact one's agenda is vital management practice, particularly at the cabinet level.

Commissioner Akins mentioned accommodating the culture:

> Most of these guys, these old politicos out in the county, all they want is a little dignity. Really, they will come in and you will see them, they will interrupt if you are in a meeting. . . . That you will actually stop what you are doing and walk outside and say "hi" to him and slap him on the back and say, "See ya." That's all he wants. A lot of people won't give that and they are wrong for not. I mean, I like to because most of these guys, I got to know them, and because I got to know them, I like them. It's a lot easier to do it when you feel like there is a personal friendship to these people.

The more central the threatened value, the more resistant the culture to the change (Rokeach 1970). Building a personal bond reduces resistance to the policy.

Governor Alexander took for granted that his managers would respect the core values present in their cultural environment. By respecting these deep-seated values, the environment will more likely tolerate the manager's organizational changes that challenge other, less strongly held values. Harold Bradley, a corrections commissioner with a national background and reputation, joined the Alexander team at the beginning of the first term, but Bradley did not accommodate the culture, and thus left. Bradley's forthright style was not a good fit with the state's cultural environment.

Organizational Factors

Decisions are affected by practices within the organization, such as the willingness of the superior to share responsibility with the subordinate. An organization can centralize control in the governor's office or distribute the authority to the department heads, as Alexander did. Each cabinet member can in turn share authority with subordinates or hold tightly to power and authority. A middle manager may have sole responsibility for a program or an activity, or share responsibility for that activity with subordinates. Alexander granted decision latitude to his cabinet; cabinet members were more restrictive toward their middle managers. Because of their limited experience with the agency, cabinet members rarely knew their subordinates well, and perhaps as a result they were reluctant to share authority.

Middle managers have substantial responsibility but limited authority. Their authority in a particular situation often is shared with other middle managers, or their recommendations require approval by a superior. While middle managers can be directive toward subordinates, dealing with peers and outside stakeholders demands a facilitative management style. Position power allows executives to assert an authoritative response to a question; middle managers rarely have this authority on the issues they face. Because they so often lack authority, effective middle managers develop competence in negotiating and facilitating, obtaining support by their wits and persuasiveness, not by the power of position.

Politics and Issues

During Alexander's administration the following groups and their beliefs had an ongoing influence on the decision process: a Republican state administration emphasizing executive leadership, a Democratic Party believing in legislative primacy, civil service employees expecting to keep their jobs regardless of performance level, and the usual array of special interests that will awaken when an issue touches their areas of concern. Each manager's story describes an effort that responds to a crisis or to an initiative that challenges the status quo.

DENSITY

"Density" is a concept that we found helpful in describing and explaining a manager's decision-making behavior. "Density" attempts to capture the complexity of the middle manager's or executive's environment, and it applies to both politics and administration.[2] On a high-density issue or in a high-density environment, competing interests and individuals are active on various sides of a question in hopes of obtaining benefits or avoiding losses. In high-density managerial situations, a manager's choices are constrained by the following:

1. close supervision (the need to have decisions approved by a supervisor), or obvious external attention (the press, or public or important groups active on the issue)
2. competing views of stakeholders or legitimate authorities regarding the situation
3. being asked to develop or implement a policy that involves a variety of administrative units not under one's authority, and units reluctant to support the policy being proposed

The physical space that high-density issues occupied was the meeting: middle managers spent an inordinate amount of time in meetings.

In a low-density situation these forces impinging on a middle manager are benign. In a low-density situation a manager has been authorized wide decision latitude by the superior, is not receiving incompatible directives, and is involved in developing or implementing a policy that has broad support from those who must implement it. High density can arise from the manager's environment or from an issue the manager faces.

Environment Density

Environment density refers to the varieties and intensities of rules, roles, institutions, structure, and culture that impinge on the manager. Environment constraints can be internal or external. Internal environment constraints are reflected in administrative reporting relationships. Density is measured by the degree to which authority and responsibility are shared, and the number of parallel or superior reporting relationships. The more shared authority and reporting relationships one has, the greater the environment density. This aspect of density resembles the concept of "networks" (McGuire 2002). Environment density is a natural part of the middle manager's work life and contributes to the amount of time managers spend meeting with others in order to get things done.

Environment density differs between middle managers and executives. The middle manager work environment is characterized by circumscribed and shared authority. Making decisions ordinarily requires gaining the support or acquiescence from agencies and people over whom one has no control. The words middle managers use to describe their problem-solving activities include "inform," "sell," "consult," "build support," "coordinate," "gather opinion," "convince," "co-opt," and "negotiate." These words indicate that the middle manager may lack the power to impose a solution. "Informing," "selling," "consulting" and the rest of these activities occur in meetings, and meetings are needed to resolve high-density issues. A middle manager must persuade people at mid-level and frontline positions that a particular policy should be instituted or implemented.

A middle manager in the Department of Correction described the frustrations faced by agency personnel directors, who regularly encountered obstacles when recruiting employees. They worked collectively to reduce some of the environment density they faced.

> Personnel directors in each state agency were hampered in their recruitment efforts because they could not access the state personnel data-base. . . . We convened a task force. Took a little longer than I expected, took about six months, but finally after about six months and several committee meetings, meetings with the commissioner and assistant commissioner, staff directors

and so forth in personnel, and some other task force people participating, they all agreed, "Well, now it certainly isn't illegal to do that." [Now] they have to give us the same information the guy on the street can have . . . you can access an applicant file to see if a person has had what jobs they say they've had. Previously they were in the computer, but nobody had access to them because it was too tightly controlled. The dynamics of coming through the group really made me very, very successful. I feel good about that, it's not a very big deal kind of thing, but it really made my staff and the personnel people in our department feel good. The commissioner doesn't even know you've done that, but it's very, very satisfying.

Agency, state, or federal regulations and the management style of one's immediate superior or commissioner are the most significant components of environment density affecting middle managers. The executive who allows subordinates wide decision latitude lowers the density of the middle manager's environment; the executive who must approve each decision taken by a subordinate increases the density of the subordinate's environment. Middle manager environment constraints arise from being in the middle of the organizational structure, from interest groups seeking benefits, and from other government agencies.

A middle manager attempting to change the hospital reimbursement policy in response to a federal initiative included hospital representatives in the planning and design stages of the policy.

We know by law that the hospitals have to be involved in this process. They don't have to be the decision makers but we know if they [are unhappy] . . . they can fight hard enough and lobby hard enough to stop us at the hearing, and we won't get it done.

Should hospitals perceive themselves as shut out from the decision process, they have legal remedies to impede state action. The wise middle manager recognizes the environment density in the situation and involves the hospitals early on.

Governor Alexander offered as enticement to take the job as commissioner the absence of environment constraint. Commissioners (except for McElrath in the Department of Education) had a free hand, as long as they avoided negative publicity and kept the department within budget. However, if they could not address issues in a way that contained the ire of stakeholders, then their position was jeopardized. Commissioners faced high density from politics and issue constraints only.

Issue Density

Issue density refers to the unique interests and people that are activated around a particular issue. While environment density is constant and associated with one's position, title, and location in the organizational network, issue density is variable and is sparked when a particular issue arouses otherwise dormant stakeholders. What are the number, intensity, and strength of forces attaching themselves to a particular issue? For low-density issues the steps of the decision process model are generally distinguishable; however, for high-density issues the decision stages intertwine, weave back and forth, until the issue resolves or is abandoned. High-density issues activate a variety of interests, perhaps augmented by the larger number and/or greater intensity of participants who need to be consulted before the decision can move forward.

Managers generally chose to talk about these high-density, challenging, time-consuming issues. Low-density issues carry minimal emotional impact with the public, and stakeholders do not believe they have interests involved. Low-density issues do not require extensive involvement of the manager's network; they are less complex and take less of the manager's time. Effective middle managers work to create relationships with stakeholders and peers outside the work group. Building these relationships is necessary, because the density of the middle management network may require cooperation from those outside the work unit, over whom the middle manager has no authority.

Commissioners are not exempt from the force of issue density, even if it comes from below and within the agency. For example, because of the strong expectation that government middle managers will not be terminated, letting an employee go requires adhering to a dismissal process acceptable to the politics and issue environment. Commissioner McCullough describes how he violated the norms, and the attendant consequences.

> I was commissioner of General Services, and the governor had gotten me to come here on the basis of looking at management, how it could be better managed, and I chaired the management committee. I looked at the Department of General Services, and I felt like it needed to be streamlined. I identified seventy-five positions that needed to be done away with. I didn't ask anybody; I terminated a division director and about eight or nine people, and all hell broke loose. Good Lord, I got calls from a Republican legislator—a very good friend of mine—who said, "You fired the guy who had the best job of anybody in my county, it was the best job in the administration, and you fired him!" And I got calls from the other side saying, "You need to appoint so and so in the position, I'm glad you fired that fellow, now here's who you can appoint." Then the papers picked up on it, and I got all kinds of questions about, "Aren't you accountable, don't you feel like you have an obligation to find them something else to do?" That wasn't done right. Now, I did the right thing, but I didn't do it right . . . I was doing just what I would have done in my business in Murfreesboro.

Commissioner McCullough acted as if he were operating in a private-sector rather than a public-sector decision environment. Shortly thereafter, Hubert McCullough was promoted to commissioner of F&A, so he left that issue behind. Violating the traditional norms could mobilize state employees, an important stakeholder group. The Republican governor's cabinet would not wish them to become actively organized against an administration initiative.

In dealing outside one's agency or up one's own hierarchy, differences in perspective, differences in importance assigned to the issues in conflict, protection of turf, or just plain contrariness by someone can slow or stymie middle manager and commissioner decisions. The fluid decision process lacks clear boundaries; problem definition and decision stages melt into one another. Density is of immense concern to the government manager.

Meetings drive high-density issues through the analysis and decision-making process. The ubiquity of meetings, especially noticeable in the middle manager stories, brought environment density and politics and issue density to our attention. Middle managers are required by their location in the hierarchy to attend to superiors, peers, and subordinates and to coordinate efforts across departments and agencies. They meet with peers, clients, citizens, superiors, subordinates, businesses, contractors, federal regulators, federal funders, local officials, and public interest groups. The behavioral sign of a dense network is the frequency of meetings, telephone calls, and e-mails needed to move an issue through the policy process.

TABLE 2.1
Environment and Issue Density

Low Density	High Density
Authority to decide	Superior reviews one's decisions
Decision process more likely straightforward	Decision process convoluted
Few iterations in the decision process	Many iterations in the decision process
Decision can be made relatively quickly	Decision cannot be made quickly
Few interests involved in the process (few approvals needed)	Many interests involved in the process (many approvals needed)
Few meetings	Many meetings
Routine implementation processes	Problematic implementation processes
Rational or incremental decision	Multiple-streams decision

A low-density issue does not involve large numbers of concerned participants. Because low-density problems do not need extensive consultation, few meetings may be needed for resolution. The process conforms better to the rational model, for an observer can often separate the assessment of the alternative ways to solve the problem from the actual decision.

Although analytically environment density can be separated from politics and issue density, the two aspects of density interact, seemingly in multiplicative fashion. In a dense network, the convoluted, rambling, inclusive decision-making process was constructed by the participants as they went along. The denser the environment or issue, the more likely that the multiple streams decision model will describe the process.

Personnel Commissioner Akins describes his strategy to gain acceptance for the proposed state employee classification system. Recognizing the need to accommodate the primary stakeholders, he talked to groups of state employees and provided information to key legislators to demonstrate that their constituents working for the state would not be disadvantaged by the new classification system.

> I traveled all over the state and spoke to 10,000 state employees in about fifty meetings in a six-week period of time. There was a lot of concern among legislators, particularly John Bragg and some of these guys, about how this thing was just going to be a political thing, that Republicans would get raises and the Democrats would be screwed over. . . . [W]e brought the computer people in and were able to generate the kind of reports that we needed when we got to the selling point. We generated printouts county by county of every state employee—where they were in the current system and where they would be in the proposed system; what the current pay range was, and what we recommended the pay range to be. We organized all those and we gave John Bragg every state employee in Rutherford County. We didn't give to all 132 legislators, but we picked out the key guys like John Bragg and Doug Henry in the Senate and Speaker McWherter and the key people [in the House] and said, "Here they are, I don't know who they are, you do. You judge what we have done to them." I think that, more than anything [is the reason] it finally passed through the legislature.

Akins talked to employees and provided detailed information to legislative leaders to show that there was no hidden agenda.[3]

As a Republican governor facing a Democratically controlled House and Senate, to pass and implement legislation Alexander and his cabinet members paid attention to the Democratic legislators as well as to the core Republican support base. The governor spent considerable time touring the state to communicate his priorities to the citizens, and the commissioners talked with agency employees and citizens. The administration's goal was to make its priorities into state policy, and in order to do that in a political setting, the governor and his executives, whether consciously or unconsciously, attended to the decision environment.

Resolving a high-density issue, whether at the executive or middle level, increases the probability that the decision process will *not* proceed according to the rational or incremental decision-making model. The pulling and hauling among multiple and diverse stakeholder groups ensure that hammering out a proposal acceptable to a sufficient number of interests to gain approval in the executive or legislative arena will involve considerable meeting time. The multiple-streams imagery of shifting positions and alliances as various policy options are offered, modified, dropped, and resurrected fits most of the stories that managers told. Embedded in the hierarchy, managers in the middle lack control over others involved in their problem-solving network. A high-density issue or environment makes likely a looping, difficult-to-follow decision process in which decision stages overlap and intertwine and issues iterate.

Decisions in lower-density situations are more visible. Assessment can be separated from decision making, and the entire process may resemble the rational-comprehensive model of decision making. Low-density issues and environments allow—but do not ensure—transparency and linearity in decision making. The manager may check with colleagues, peers in other states, or a professional association for suggestions. After exploring the options, the manager selects the best available solution, clears the solution with a superior if necessary, and acts. If disagreement arises and the manager lacks the authority or willingness to act unilaterally, then the issue dies or goes to a higher level for decision.

Alexander's management system created a low-density environment for cabinet members. Alexander delegated responsibility to them to handle matters within their jurisdiction. He did not like controversy among members of the cabinet and did not look kindly upon one cabinet member attempting to poach programs from another department. He authorized department executives to act and protected them against encroaching peers. Power lay in the hands of the cabinet member; the challenge to cabinet members was not overcoming constraints on their power to decide but using wisely the considerable power they were granted.

CONCLUSIONS

We found that the dominant thinking processes of the managers and executives are nonlinear and do not conform to the decision models of rationality, satisficing, or incrementalism.[4] "Multiple-streams" theory, a variant of "garbage can" theory, seems to fit. Some problems arrived already defined.

Other situations slowed down, stopped, were shunted aside, or were recycled multiple times before decision and implementation. No stage in the process was safe from being reassessed as time passed, as the situation changed, and as new participants joined the process and veteran participants departed.

Decisions do not take place in a vacuum but within an environment incorporating the culture and values broadly shared by the people of the state, the decision structure surrounding the location of the issue, and the number and intensity of stakeholders aroused by the specific issue. The aggregate impact of cultural values, decision structure, and stakeholder size and intensity creates the variable of *density*, which influences the speed by which an issue traverses the decision process. High density occurs when issues challenge cultural norms, attract many participants attempting to influence the policy decision, and are situated structurally so that multiple authorizations are needed before a decision can be made or implemented.

In defining the problem, the more complex the situation, the less likely a rational choice approach is useful for understanding the decision process, and the more likely the social constructionist approach will account for what is observed. The manager constructs a problem from the issue in question, then proceeds to work out a solution. Forcing a high-profile decision embedded in a complex environment into the rational model can give a false positive reading regarding the utility of the rational model. High-profile issues in dense environments are better seen as constructed than identified, and the construction/solution/implementation process oscillates until the manager locks onto a construction/solution/implementation set that seems to work. High density contributes to an iterative, opaque decision process in which stages overlap and intertwine, and challenge the manager who attempts to move a policy or program through the decision system.

Low-density issues lack these pressures. Resolving an issue in a low-density environment may proceed according to the standard, rational decision model, allowing transparency and linearity in decision making. Those routine situations are less exciting or challenging to outstanding managers. Density is sometimes predictable due to the location of the issue within the administrative system or nature of the issue, but density also can arise unexpectedly, can grind normal processes to a halt, and can consume the attention of a middle manager or an executive.

Managers and executives differed in their approaches to situations. Governor Alexander's decentralized management system provided commissioners with a low-density structure in which to manage. Because their structural environment was less dense, commissioners had the authority to decide many matters unilaterally. In the stories they chose to tell, middle managers rarely had such authority, because although commissioners frequently involved subordinates in policy decisions, commissioners tended not to allow middle managers to make decisions independently.

We used the four-stage model to organize the material in this book because the individual elements of the model were a useful vehicle to present the activities of the managers and executives in the stories they narrated. The next four chapters detail how commissioners and middle managers faced the issues during the various aspects of the decision process. Ordinarily, the chapter on methods used in the study would be included either within or following the present chapter. However, because of the long discussion of density and because our methods discussion also is extensive, reviewers suggested moving the chapter on methods so that we could more quickly reach the theoretical and substantive issues. Interested readers are invited to visit the Appendix at this point, or to continue to chapter 3, "Problem Identification."

THREE

Problem Identification

To A CABINET MEMBER the challenge of identifying the problem can begin even before formally assuming the job. Commissioner Sammie Lynn Puett describes an incident that happened on the day she was sworn in as commissioner for the Department of Human Services.

As I rode down the elevator to be sworn in, this man, who at that time was serving as deputy in the department, pulls a news release out of his pocket and he says, "I've just written this news release to say that we're calling off the mail issuance of food stamps in Knox County." This was on the 28th day of January, and my term began on February the 1st. I said, "Who have you talked to about this?"

"Nobody, I'm just gonna put this out."

I said, "You haven't talked to any of the people in this department, you haven't talked to Knox County about it, you haven't talked to our systems and procedures where we're generating this, haven't talked with the family assistance person?"

"No."

I couldn't believe that we were about to undo 16,000 food stamp recipients who thought they were gonna get their food stamps in the mail. . . . I had to learn real fast. . . . [T]he end result was I fired that guy not long after. Absolutely unreal, I don't know whether he was setting me up or what. I still don't understand. I don't think so, I don't think he was smart enough to, I think that was just the way he operated . . . I didn't know who to trust. The department was in such a mess, [I didn't know] who was out there building a fire and striking a match. About the time you blew that one out, somebody had lit a fire someplace else, it was really an unreal situation.

How do managers identify the issues or problems that will constitute their managerial and policy agendas? How do top executives differ from middle managers in how they decide what needs to be done? What needs to be done? What seems to be the problem? What are the pressing issues? What should we be doing? Are we neglecting an important task? The answers to these questions will determine the content of the work that the executives and managers perform, and that is the focus of this chapter. We will show how state executives and managers identify the situations that constitute their managerial and policy agendas and illustrate how executives differ from middle managers.

PROBLEM IDENTIFICATION/AGENDA SETTING

The decision-making process commences with problem identification, or "agenda setting" (Anderson 2006, ch. 3; Baumgartner and Jones 1993; Durant 1998; Kingdon 1984; Lester and Stewart 2000; Rochefort and Cobb 1994).[1] We name the things to which we will attend and frame the context in which we will attend to them (Schon 1983). An unlimited number of problems and opportunities are floating in the environment waiting to be addressed. Once a problem is selected and defined, a limited range of possible solutions attaches to it. The subjectivity of managerial problem identification suggests that the concept of a "Type III error"—solving the wrong problem (Raiffa 1968)—needs refining.[2] In technical work there is a wrong problem. Managerial work is different from technical work. The notion of the "wrong problem" in managerial work is the perspective of someone using a different problem definition ("My interpretation of the political environment does not support that definition of the problem"), or personally disagreeing ("I would offer an alternative definition of the problem"). Mitroff (1998, 9) says that all management mistakes can be traced to one fundamental flaw: solving the wrong problem precisely. This "frame blindness" is described by Russo and Schoemaker (1989) as the inability to visualize multiple conceptions of the same situation.

The problem identification process has received more attention in policy studies than in administrative studies. By defining an issue in a particular way, policy activists attempt to steer an issue into an arena sympathetic to their interests. By putting their interpretation on a situation, the politician, party, or interest group seeks by framing the issue in a particular way to gain favorable public opinion toward their interpretation. Schattschneider (1960) argued that the ability to define the arena created an opportunity to control the outcome. By controlling problem identification activists seek to determine the arena, thereby increasing the probability of an outcome to their liking. Rochefort and Cobb (1994) offer a collection of readings demonstrating the usefulness of agenda setting to understanding policy making in air transportation, ground traffic congestion, drugs, AIDS, and agriculture.

Perhaps the lack of attention to administrative agenda setting or problem identification is attributable to a perceived "politics-administration dichotomy." Elected officials make policy; administrators implement policy. The politics-administration dichotomy is a partial truth. Elected officials make policy, but they may also involve themselves in implementation by micromanaging. Administrators cannot avoid influencing policy as they implement the legislation handed them by elected officials. Politics and administration are distinct and separate, but also entwined.

A "problem" or an "opportunity" has life only if it is so identified by someone with sufficient influence to direct attention toward that situation. Defining a problem sets boundaries to our attention and imposes coherence on a situation, which allows us to say what is wrong and how this situation should be changed.[3] Managerial problems are in the eye of the beholder—they are subjectively defined. By focusing the attention of participants on a particular "problem," the manager may eliminate other "problems" from rising onto the action agenda.

The administrative problem identification process inside an agency does not receive extensive public or research attention, but problem identification is a daily activity for the public manager. The range of managerial problems visible to a manager or executive is a function of the individual's position in the hierarchy, one's perspective, and the political environment surrounding the manager or executive. The manager's agenda is malleable, affected by political activity in the environment and influenced by the individual's personal motivation and ability to act. *Position, politics,* and *perspective* are important factors when accounting for the issues that will take priority on the manager's agenda, the issues the manager selects to address, and how the manager defines those issues.

Position

The importance of position, one's location in the formal organization, is readily understood and acknowledged by both practitioners and scholars. Hierarchy is widely perceived to govern administrative decision making, with the Weberian legal-rational administrative system as the presumptive model. Decisions are taken at the top of the organization. Orders trickle down the hierarchy—one tells another, who tells another, until implementation occurs. Having a high position grants discretion to set a broader agenda, thus to define the problems that will constitute the agenda for subordinates. A commissioner, who reports to the governor, sets the agency's agenda with reasonable assurance that the issue will command attention and instigate action within the agency.

Issues enter at various locations in the hierarchy, and each position has its own issue concerns. Every management level has areas in which authoritative pronouncements can be made. Middle managers have narrower responsibilities and less control over their agendas than do executives. A middle manager must expend effort to import an issue that is not embedded in one's job description or routine duties. A commissioner has more latitude than a middle manager in selecting, interpreting, and deciding issues. The following story of a promoted middle manager illustrates the importance of position and how location in the hierarchical structure colors an individual's perception of organizational problems.

> I was working as warden and it had come to my attention that the prison hospital needed a particular piece of equipment. We desperately needed this piece of equipment. I wrote an eight-page memo detailing all the reasons why we had to have this thing. I couldn't see how they could turn us down at the central office; this was critical to the operations of the medical facility. Well, I wrote the memo on a Thursday, and that Friday I got a promotion and I was moved to the central office. I moved on Tuesday. On Wednesday, I received my own memo. I had to turn myself down.

Participatory management and consultative decision making have become pervasive in the management literature, but such counter-hierarchical notions appear to have shallow roots in management practice. The middle manager's and executive's organizational positions influence significantly the issues they face and the problems they identify. Position is an important factor in shaping a manager's agenda and defining a problem.

Politics

Politics is the visible clash of preferences—politicians seeking favorable publicity for reelection plans or benefits for friends and supporters, organized interests pursuing their goals, and amorphous public opinion stating value preferences. Politics compels government employees to respond to articulated demands coming from outside the unit or agency. In state government, as in all governments, there is no fixed goal toward which the government is heading; consequently, there are no clearly identifiable, easily agreed upon policy or managerial problems to be solved. The emerging issues result from events in the environment and the political preferences of the significant decision makers and stakeholders. The bargaining-compromise-accommodation process of politics shapes the issues that make up the public agenda. Defining the problem is a political process (Dunn 1981; Stone 1988; Jones 1994). When a significant stakeholder brings an issue touching on the agency's content area into

the public arena, a manager's political antennae are fully extended, and problem identification becomes politicized.

Getting on the manager's agenda via politics depends on the strength of the
issue's supporters, not the righteousness of the cause. Public agencies are rife with
issues that never make it onto the agenda for action. In the political context, concerns languish unless the issue champion is able to rally sufficient support to ele-
vate the issue to the status of "problem that merits attention." Politics can ener-
gize any issue and force it to the top of the manager's agenda. Executives deal
with partisan politics as a component of the problem identification process.

Middle managers were largely insulated from partisan political issues.
Interest groups with competing aims were the political actors confronted by
middle managers. Interest group conflicts may pit two sections of an agency
against each other (patient advocates versus nursing home owners in the
Department of Health), or two departments against each other (Department
of Health versus Department of Agriculture in carrying out food inspections).
Politics intrudes in the middle managers' problem identification process differently than it does for the executives.

Perspective

Perspective, determined by one's personality, background, and experience, is
the invisible choice that individuals make about what matters and what does
not, what should be attended to and what can be ignored. Unlike politics,
which is visible and obvious, perspective involves the individual's personal
biases that, consciously or unconsciously, drive the selection of an issue for
attention. Personal preferences, educational background and training, and
prior work experiences influence the way a manager or an executive looks at a
situation. An engineer tends to see problems or solutions in terms of something to be built, while a lawyer will be sensitive to the legal process. Department of Transportation Commissioner Farris, whose primary career experience was in retailing, chose inventory as a managerial issue, whereas
Commissioner Sansom, who headed the same department but came from an
engineering background, emphasized monitoring highway construction. Perspective influences what a manager finds in a situation, the priorities toward
which one chooses to direct one's attention.

To summarize, an issue gains the attention of the manager for one of
three reasons:

1. Position: because the issue falls within the responsibility of the manager's
   position
2. Politics: because politics has forced the issue onto the manager's agenda
3. Perspective: because the manager has a personal desire to address the situation

"Position" and "politics" impose issues on the manager. "Perspective" describes those situations in which the manager's personal agenda dominates. We will first present these activities of middle managers, then turn to executives.

MIDDLE MANAGERS

The stories middle managers tell illustrate what they believe to be significant challenges, and they cover a wide spectrum of accomplishment. Although middle managers' activities have a broad range, their actions do not have the far-reaching impact of the actions taken by commissioners. Middle managers tell stories of coordination, reorganization, technical innovation, conflict resolution, and implementation. Middle managers do not work directly for the governor, and they cannot change the direction of their departments. Middle managers have less latitude than do executives to choose problems on which to work. Issues usually arise elsewhere and travel to the middle manager's desk. Subordinates push problems up the chain of command; superiors send issues down to the middle manager for action; and peers from other agencies contact the middle manager with their wishes and concerns.

Position: Problems Sent through Channels

Challenges can come to the middle manager's desk from below, from above, or from outside the agency. Problems that originate outside and land on the manager's desk through official channels of communication are not easily ignored. Someone along the bureaucratic chain thinks that the particular issue is a problem that needs attention. Once the problem is put on the action agenda, even if the problem starts out on someone else's action agenda, the middle manager is ill-advised to ignore it. The ball has been put in one's court; a failure to act reflects negatively on one's competence.

It comes as no surprise that subordinates channel troublesome problems up the line for the middle manager to handle. Nor is it surprising that the superior refers problems down to the middle manager's desk. The middle manager faces downward toward subordinates, upward toward the executive, and horizontally to peers in other agencies who have problems they would like to get rid of. One manager was sent a problem from her subordinates regarding clarification and equalization of the procedures to admit clients to state mental health facilities. After working with peers in related organizations, this mental health middle manager felt that the problem of clarifying and equalizing the procedures for admitting clients had been festering too long. It had been a source of irritation to managers in related organizations. Peers encouraged her to tackle the issues.

> Originally the problem came out of the planning process . . . (but) when the community could get someone in for evaluation easier than for treatment, the system began to boil over. I started writing a series of memos saying . . . we need to be able to identify services for these individuals. . . . Along about that time my counterpart in community services started identifying more gaps in the mental health centers.

This manager received the communication from peers outside the agency, which resonated with her personal feelings, and she chose to take action.

Two middle managers received an assignment from the commissioner of safety:

> When they first passed photo drivers' licenses, there was a big rush to get the program put together. . . . They were having a lot of complaints from driver's license people. . . . The governor's office received more complaints from that area than any other area in state government. Of course, Commissioner Roberts was alarmed about that, and he decided that we needed to do something. He assigned Charles and me to go out to see what was wrong and see what we could do about it.

Their charge required both identifying the problem and solving it. The problem traveled from the governor's office to the commissioner, to these two middle managers, who were sent on special assignment to work full time to define this problem and then solve it.

Another middle manager was encouraged to deal with a problem that was identified by a federal support agency, the National Institute of Corrections (NIC). The federal agency had been called in originally to assist the department in designing a classification system and workload analysis program. After looking over the situation, the federal agency declined to provide that requested service. Instead, it offered its organizational development expertise to assist the agency in coping with "the spirit of intrigue" that pervaded the working unit.

> They [NIC] said, "Tell you what we'll do. We won't come in and set up classification for you, and we won't do a workload analysis system with you. But we will come in and do some organizational development with you. We will help you and your group do it. Because if you don't do that, it won't do any good to get you a case management system. Your organization needs this first before anything else can come down."

The negative climate was identified by outside observers and brought to the manager's attention. The outside organization convinced him to define organizational climate as a problem. Once the problem was identified, the manager went to great lengths to improve his unit's decision-making processes.

The governor, desiring to cut red tape, issued an executive order to all agencies to eliminate duplicate services. An assistant commissioner in the Department of Agriculture tells the story about identifying this problem, which was set in motion by the governor's message, and soon attracted into the discussion those businesses that sold food products, as well as middle managers and stakeholders from the state agencies that inspect food products.

> Stores were concerned about being inspected two or three times a year by the same standard by two different departments. The governor, getting into the second administration, issued an executive order. It was his intention to eliminate all duplication by state government. So, we realized the duplication and the grocery store industry realized the duplication, and we all started to eliminate all of that.

This issue was identified by the governor's office, traveled to the agencies, then down to an assistant commissioner's desk, attracting the involvement of interest groups along the way. Problem identification was not contentious; all parties agreed that duplicate inspections should be halted.

All of the previous situations landed on a middle manager's desk by referral from peers, superiors, or subordinates. Position in the hierarchy largely dictated that the problem would land on that particular manager's desk.

Perspective

Some middle managers discussed interpersonal office problems that they personally felt interfered with doing an effective job. These stories described personnel disagreements, interpersonal conflicts, unsupportive and uncooperative group relations, or high levels of mistrust in a work unit.

A negative work environment, identified by the manager alone, without involvement of a superior, is often seen as a problem that needs to be addressed. A recently appointed agency personnel director thus described her situation:

> The managers were receiving absolutely no response from personnel [section within the agency] at all. . . . It was a wonder they were getting paid. There was a great deal of misinformation, a lot of suspicion between the department managers and the administration.

Having succeeded another manager in the same department who did not choose to define the work climate or interpersonal conflict as a problem, the manager identified the negative work environment as what she chose to handle.

Another middle manager went against the advice of those around her. She took a chance on hiring an overeducated analyst who had negative evaluations in his personnel file.

The person who was highest on the register was extremely overqualified for the job . . . this person had a PhD and years of teaching experience. He came in for the interview. I was very impressed with him. . . . We ordered his file from personnel. It was full of one problem after another. He had a history of problems, lawsuits, and this sort of thing; one of them, for instance, was that his job was abolished and he lobbied hard to have the position not abolished. He had in his hand a letter of commendation saying, "This guy is great, rehire him for any kind of state job," then in his file is this conflicting document coming from his former boss saying "No, don't rehire him; he's a jerk."

Many managers would likely have routinely eliminated this applicant from the pool, thus an issue would never have arisen. That was the advice she received from her superior, who disagreed with, but did not oppose, her decision to hire the individual. Because many managers would never have considered hiring the individual in the first place, they would never have seen or grappled with this issue. This "problem" employee gave the department several good years, and then went off to a teaching career in higher education. The manager was proud that she was able not only to provide a good employee to the state but also to rehabilitate the reputation of a capable individual.

The aforementioned middle managers went against the flow in the problems they chose to address. Not all managers entering an ineffective work environment will perceive it as such, and if they do, they may not choose to go against the decision environment by taking remedial action, nor will the usual manager take the risk of hiring someone with negative comments in his or her resume.

One middle manager, who faced opposition from his superior, describes how he maintained his pilot program in fire protection.

I had to use my personal relationship with them [the fire chiefs] to keep them from backing out of the project because they got nothing out of it. They were filling out the forms and mailing them in, but they were not getting anything back. . . . It was just a matter of a personal relationship with some of them. Most of them, in fact, all the ten pilots [pilot projects] except one, hung in there just by my personal assurances. I kept telling them that someday we'll have some support from upper level management, and then this project will get up and go.

This middle manager went beyond his job description to identify a problem and to convince others that the project was worth doing. He kept the project on the policy agenda.

These managers identified problems that would not have been identified by another manager if that manager had simply been working within the confines of the job description, the expectations of the decision environment, or a superior's orders. In the case of the fire chief's program that faced a hostile agency head, the manager could have just let the program fall by the wayside. These managers studied the situations, took risks, and provided enhanced value to the citizens of Tennessee.

Issues and problems self-identified by middle managers ranged from important only to the unit that housed the manager, to minor innovation, to major change. The number of people that needed to be convinced that the problem merited attention increased as the impact of the change affected people and work units further afield from the manager's own department. In all cases the manager's initiative put the issue on the agenda, thereby creating the problem definition. Another manager in the same situation may not have identified the situation as an issue or problem to be addressed.

Position, Politics, and Perspective in the Middle of the Organization

The middle manager's ability or personal willingness to identify problems is constrained by position in the hierarchy. Regular duties are prescribed, and the job description limits discretion. Tasks within the job description usually are clearly stated and offer limited problem identification latitude. Going against the cultural expectation increases the manager's risk. Assignments and opportunities coming from outside the agency may offer variety, and perhaps some problem identification discretion.

Partisan politics was invisible in the middle managers' problem identification activities. Politics is influenced by their clients' perspectives and demands for service, but general public opinion does not influence middle managers' selection of issues. If a significant political actor lobbied for policy action in a middle manager's area of responsibility, then the middle manager would be aware of the demand for change but would not make the decision on whether to address the issue or to favor one problem definition over another. Partisan demands appear *not* to influence problem identification by middle managers.

"Perspective" is harder to grasp. Self-identified issues are limited in scope by the middle manager's location in the hierarchy. Commitment to doing a good job motivated some middle managers to tackle problems that previous middle managers had ignored. A middle manager's individual preferences can influence which problems get addressed and which do not. The several examples of a middle manager choosing to consider a situation a significant problem needing a solution illustrate how subjective construction of problems occurs at the middle manager level.

Position is the primary motivator in middle manager problem identification. Politics affects middle managers indirectly—issues that descend from above may have a political component, but partisan politics does not appear to affect directly the problem definition choices for the middle managers we studied. Their heavy agenda and constrained job description limits their opportunity to exercise "perspective."

EXECUTIVES

Commissioners told significantly longer stories than did middle managers. Their narratives were embellished by vignettes and side stories filled with complications and intricacies. Although commissioners are not known to most citizens, as executives of state government departments they have a widespread and significant impact on the rules, regulations, and quality of life of the state's citizens.

Unless Governor Alexander expressed an interest in the department and its agenda, the commissioner was unrestricted in determining which situations received attention. On the campaign trail prior to his first term, Alexander promised to reduce the number of state employees. This task was delegated to Lewis Donelson, commissioner of F&A, who relished the challenge. Halfway through the first term, and into the second term, education became Alexander's priority. Because education reform demanded overcoming entrenched interests and raising taxes to pay for the reform, Alexander weighed in heavily to define the problem and mobilize support. Education commissioner McElrath spoke of working closely with the governor in fleshing out the state's agenda for education.

Other commissioners were left alone, having almost unlimited authority to identify problems and set their agendas. Bob Farris, upon accepting his responsibility as commissioner of the Department of Transportation, recalled that Governor Alexander said, "Do a good job. If I have anything, I will call you. You will hear from me occasionally. You just go and do a good job." Farris went on to say that the governor had chosen education as the important issue for Tennessee, therefore it was up to him, Farris, to manage and direct the transportation department. This wide-ranging mandate to create an agenda for the department was echoed by the commissioners. Within the broad mandate of doing what needed to be done, the commissioners' attention ranged from internal organization management to national policy.

Most commissioners were unfamiliar with their subordinates and with the organization, yet commissioners did not report seeking advice on agenda setting or problem definition from subordinates. Their usual contacts were with their predecessors, fellow commissioners, or friends. Most of these executives had obtained their government appointments because they were successful managers in other venues, so they had the self-confidence to figure out and act on what needed to be done. Problems reached the commissioners' agendas by being linked to the governor's program, by the commissioner identifying problems that needed to be addressed, by issues forcing their way onto the commissioner's agenda from the bureaucracy below, or from the legislature. Issues identified by the commissioner fit comfortably into the categories of position, politics and perspective.

Position: Governor Heavily Involved

In his run for reelection, the governor's primary platform plank was a specific proposal to reform education, so the Department of Education was bound by that campaign promise. Commissioner McElrath told of the educational reform efforts, and his story illustrates a different picture than any other cabinet member regarding the role of the governor in policy making. The "education problem" was identified by the governor. The commissioner joined the team composed of the governor, his staff, and outside experts, with a mission to design, market, and implement a comprehensive package of educational reform. McElrath was the only commissioner who used the pronoun "we," referring to the governor and himself, in the story he told.[4]

In education, problem identification was the governor's initiative. The governor acted as chief educational policy maker, and he defined the problem. McElrath said:

> I think all of us agreed that we felt that our children were just as intelligent as the children in the other forty-nine states, and yet we didn't have favorable rankings in terms of student achievement, and we just couldn't buy that, we couldn't accept it.

The commissioner acted as the liaison between the Department of Education and outside educational experts in creating the plan, and he involved himself with selling the plan to the legislature, to school boards, and to teachers. But since education was the governor's central policy focus, the commissioner's problem identification activities were more limited than any other cabinet member. The governor took the lead in defining and focusing public attention in this area; the commissioner was a member of the governor's team.

Position: Governor Minimally Involved

Reducing the number of state employees was the centerpiece of Alexander's first election campaign. Not a policy initiative in the sense that the direction of government was to change; rather, this promise focused on efficient administration of the state. Defining the problem required identifying places in government where cuts could be made while maintaining service quality. This was a management problem, not a policy problem. Carrying out that campaign promise fell to the commissioner of F&A, Lewis Donelson, who said:

> It was a campaign promise of the governor, . . . the governor and I agreed that there were probably too many people working for the state. I wanted to . . . pay people better and have fewer of them.

The promise of a free hand in accomplishing the material reduction in the state payroll was the incentive used by Alexander to entice Donelson to join his cabinet. The governor had identified a problem to which Donelson was strongly committed. Having successfully recruited Donelson, the governor turned specific problem identification, solution, and implementation over to him. Many governors make promises to reduce government. Alexander was fortunate to have a strong manager, Donelson, with the desire and the ability to accomplish the reduction.

Alexander consciously removed himself from the specifics of budget reduction so that he was more insulated from pressures to provide a service to a constituency or relief to a cabinet member. He committed to supporting Donelson's decisions. Donelson recalled Governor Alexander saying:

> "I'll back you up 100 percent." That's why I never worried about him over-ruling me. Occasionally, he would have to tell a commissioner that he did not overrule me. That was really more in the beginning. We met with several commissioners and he said, "Lewie is running with that, it is going to be virtually impossible for you to get in to see me about it. Deal with him. Get your problems settled with him."

Donelson described Alexander's vision:

> He wanted to have the budget grow less than inflation, to materially reduce the state payroll, and he wanted to reduce the debt. Those were my real assignments, and basically his commitment to me was, "Whatever you have to do, do; I'll back you up."

Donelson assembled a task force dominated by cabinet members with business executive experience. The governor attended the first meeting of the task force and laid out his goals for this reduction. From that point onward, fulfilling this campaign promise was the responsibility of the F&A commissioner. Donelson planned and implemented the governor's promise: "I wanted to improve the pay and reduce the payroll." Note that Donelson uses the pronoun "I." Donelson was in charge of budget cutting; cutting administrative costs and increasing pay were not a team effort led by the governor. On the other hand, Department of Education Commissioner McElrath used the pronoun "we" when discussing his relationship to the governor. McElrath was not in charge of the education initiative. In reducing the state payroll, the governor outlined a broad goal, but the problem was defined and then the process directed by Donelson. Donelson cited this effort as "the most managerially demanding thing that I did when I was commissioner."

Perspective: Commissioner Identified the Problem
and Convinced the Governor to Go Along

A firm believer in a strong education system, Commissioner Donelson (degrees from Choate, Rhodes, and Georgetown Law School) also believed that the University of Tennessee at Knoxville (UTK) needed to raise its standards to establish itself as a major state university and to distinguish itself from other state-supported schools. He tested his idea with a large group of administrators from UTK; naturally, his audience enthusiastically supported his proposal.

> Before I told Jack Reese [UTK chancellor] that I could actually do it . . . I made a big speech at that meeting [department heads' retreat] about raising the standards, how UTK needed to get into the business of quality education and leave some of these other jobs to East Tennessee State and other places like that. The guys there absolutely loved it. They ate it with a spoon. Jack could sense that, and he was rolling with the tide.

Having received positive and public affirmation, Donelson leveraged this support, however contrived, to create a plan. He proposed that UTK receive the same amount of money the university had received the year before if Chancellor Reese agreed to raise the academic standards, which would reduce enrollment. When Donelson and Reese had general agreement on the policy, but before any formal decisions were made, Donelson approached the governor for his support. Donelson indicated that this was a policy issue. As he put it, "To what extent are we going to fund things, that was the kind of thing I would take to the governor. . . . [I would take] anything that I thought had serious political ramifications for him."

This issue was raised by Donelson, not the governor. Donelson selected the problem, floated a trial balloon to generate support (the audience for the trial balloon was biased to support the proposal), and then took the situation to the governor. Donelson convinced the governor, and Alexander supported this decision of his chief administrator. Given agreement on the problem, the solution was easy to agree on and to implement. However, it was Donelson who identified the original problem based on his personal view of education and the role of the state's flagship university.

Position: Problem Originating Below in the Bureaucracy

Commissioners, like middle managers, are confronted with problems that come from below in the bureaucracy, problems that must be faced. The buck stops at the commissioner's office. An assistant commissioner in the Department of Human Services (DHS) asked for the resignation of a counselor and a county director of social services because of seemingly grossly unprofessional conduct surrounding a child sexual abuse case. Commissioner Sammie Lynn Puett was informed by her staff of the action that had been taken. As word of the resignations spread, the commissioner was pulled into the controversy. Sorting through the differing interpretations of the situation became the commissioner's problem.

> We thought that this was the worst professional judgment in action that we had seen. We got those resignations, I had them in hand about the time my phone started ringing about this horrible DHS that was about to fire two long-time employees. . . . We had all the newspapers trying to find out what we were doing to these two poor employees. But the confidentiality of the records [was involved] . . . the juvenile judge there was the former father-in-law of this girl . . . I had never heard of anything as complicated in my life. . . . The governor's office was getting telephone calls. . . . It was really hard to sort out the facts of the situation, what really happened, what didn't happen.

The central element in the case was the suspected sexual abuse of a child by family members, but observers had divergent views of the situation. The professional DHS staffers saw the problem as maintaining professional standards, and they were demanding that those employees be fired. Other DHS employees, less informed and further from the situation, saw the problem as "the state office won't back you up if you happen to make a wrong decision." The local legislators saw the situation as a problem of interface between their constituency and the state bureaucracy, so two state representatives transported the fired social workers to the commissioner's office. The situation had further partisan potential because the director who was asked to resign was a daughter-in-law of the Republican Party state chairman. The local community "was up in arms because these were just great people" who were being fired, and "nobody in town thought that there was anything wrong with what had been done." The governor's office was being contacted by local citizens. The newspapers viewed the situation as a news story, but the ability to tell the state's side was limited by issues of the confidentiality of the records and maintaining the child's privacy.

The commissioner faced a range of plausible problem definitions from important constituencies of her department. Her challenge was deciding among the definitions. Had the controversy not emerged, she would likely have accepted the professional opinion in the department, that the social workers should resign. What was defined initially as a problem of poor judgment by department employees, to be dealt with at the middle manager level, erupted into a situation that landed on the commissioner's desk because hers was the administrative position at the apex of the pyramid; the commissioner could not avoid the problem.

Perspective: The Governor Uninvolved and Largely Unaware

Bob Farris, commissioner of the Department of Transportation, was asked about Alexander's involvement in setting the department's agenda.

> He doesn't come over here and mess with my department. . . . About once a
> year we sit down and I go through the program priorities that I am about to
> develop and I'll explain 'em and he'll ask me questions. If he has some com-
> ment he makes it, most of the time he doesn't. He does that with all the
> departments, but he'll focus on certain select things, as a governor ought to do.

Commissioner Hubert McCullough, commissioner of F&A after Lewis Donelson and Bill Sansom, characterized his situation similarly.

> The governor and I have a pretty good understanding. I go about running
> the government, and he goes about doing those things that make Tennessee
> a better state. . . . Or, I'll say it another way because I don't want to come up
> sounding presumptuous or anything like that: we understand our roles. I
> understand what he wants me to do, and I go about doing it. We don't waste
> a lot of conversation about it.

The extensive discretion to decide their own agendas for their departments, coupled with the governor's limited agenda, meant that the commissioners had broad discretion to identify the problems that their departments
would address without consulting the governor.

Perspective: Commissioner Identified
Based on Past Experiences with Government

Prior to becoming commissioner, Susan Simons had dealings with the
Department of General Services by serving as the procurement officer in
another agency. She related how a computer that she had requested had been
held up by the Department of General Services for eighteen months.

> It was my perception that this [Department of General Service's control ori-
> entation] was their major problem, and it did not take long after listening to
> other people to confirm that my perception was correct. This is a control
> agency, and it has no right to be a control agency. It is a service agency, and
> that is the way it would most effectively service state government.

Having identified the problem from her own experience, and then having that
perception reinforced by her colleagues, she decided early that changing the
Department of General Services from a control agency to a support agency
was her mission. Her decision to attack this problem rather than other possi-

ble problems in the department was a personal one. The governor had appointed her to do a job, and she felt free to proceed to act as she saw fit.

Department of Personnel Commissioner Martha Olsen also approached her new position from a perspective outside of the department she was administering. She gained experience in her former position, commissioner of revenue.

> I did not want to make the same mistake I'd made in the Department of Revenue—not doing early on what I sensed needed to be done. . . . So I worked early on to ask the experts in our organization confidentially to begin to look at the organization.

Commissioner Olsen saw the organization "set up as a result of people and not the functional aspects of the organization. It wasn't an efficient organization." Olsen succeeded another commissioner of personnel interviewed for this project, Darrell Akins. Akins took on the challenge of initiating a large-scale reclassification project. To accomplish that task, he shuffled responsibilities among his top administrative staff to match people's skills with the reclassification task demands. One executive's effective structure was defined as a problem by the following executive. The task at hand is seen through the prism of one's past experiences. The ideal meshing of tasks for efficiency to one commissioner became a totally mixed up organization to his successor, a problem that had to be fixed.

Perspective: Commissioner Identified by Walking Around

Two commissioners indicated that they had accepted the position as department head without any preconceived notions of the problems facing the department. Both commissioners headed the Department of Transportation, so their definition of problems facing the department expands on the subjectivity of problem identification.

Commissioner Farris had a background in sales and marketing; he lacked road-building experience. To become knowledgeable regarding issues facing the department he talked to people throughout the organization, spent time reading the reports generated by the different divisions, and visited work sites. He did this to "define our problems, both organizationally and programmatically." Early on he identified an inventory problem.

> I was making my initial tour of my garages and going through the warehouses. In the warehouse I noticed a stack of air filters covered with dust. I went out and blew the dust off, and it was an air filter for the Ford Edsel. I don't know how many Edsels we had at the time. . . . The guy there had ordered twenty-four filters because they came twenty-four to a case. And they are still there.

Suspecting inventory as a problem, Farris began to delve more deeply. By examining inventory and requisition forms he confirmed his suspicion that the problem extended beyond the one particular garage and included excessive use of some DOT supplies. For instance, water coolers were replaced four times more frequently in one field office than the others. It would appear that the coolers were walking. To Farris, excessive inventory, ineffectively monitored purchasing, was a significant agency problem that needed to be addressed.

Bill Sansom joined the Department of Transportation with an engineering background but also without any sense of the state's key transportation problems. He drove the highway system among the major cities in Tennessee, "and it became clear pretty quickly that route I-440 was the number one challenge in Nashville." Having identified this section of road as a problem, Samson began to investigate the court case that had halted the construction.

Both Farris and Sansom oversaw the same department, but to hear them describe the Department of Transportation, you would not be so sure. They chose identical strategies—"walking around"—to discover the principal initiatives needed in the department, but the two commissioners saw totally different agency priorities. The lenses they used to identify pressing issues derived from what made them successful in their prior careers—controlling inventory for Farris and speeding stalled construction projects for Sansom.

Hubert McCullough and Lewis Donelson were both commissioners of F&A. Raising UTK's admission standards was identified by Donelson based on his own interest in higher education.[5] Commissioner McCullough, a businessman with property investments, indicated that "when I got there I made a list of a dozen things that I thought that I wanted as commissioner of finance." One that he chose to talk about was to manage better the physical space of government, a problem that had been around for years. He chose as a priority a project directly related to an area in which he had expertise.

> I thought the state leased an inordinate amount of space . . . [this problem] was not even creative thought on my part, but it had been talked about. Senator Motlow, former senator and now dead, had great building plans but they just never got off the ground. So I don't take any credit for having thought about it, perhaps I had a little something to do with getting it started and getting it on track.

These problems did not demand the involvement of the governor. Executives picked these topics based upon their backgrounds and experience. Engineers see engineering problems. Retailers see inventory problems. People with experience in property management are sensitive to efficient planning for the use of physical space.

Politics: Legislator Involvement in Problem Identification

The legislative branch was involved in the child abuse case described earlier with DHS because a legislator accompanied the accused state workers to the commissioner's office. However, that was the extent of legislator involvement. The legislator provided access to the department head for his constituents. All legislators perform this constituency service function in order to maintain and cultivate electoral support in the district. To the extent that legislator involvement influenced the commissioner's definition of the problem, it did so only to ensure that the workers' side of the story was told to the person who would ultimately make the decision on their fate. Also, the legislature was involved in the education proposal in which Governor Alexander took an active role.

An individual legislator also was mentioned in Commissioner McCullough's story about expanding the building plan for the state. McCullough resurrected a dormant plan, authored originally by a state senator, for constructing state office buildings. McCullough's linking his proposal to Senator Motlow's communicated that this problem was identified by the legislature earlier, thereby seeking to broaden sponsorship of the building plan.

Individual legislators can shape the way the problem reaches the table for discussion. Commissioner Word, Department of Health, told about dealing with a problem of poor nursing home care that was identified by a legislator. The commissioner distinguished "representative" politics from "partisan" politics. In the commissioner's view, the nursing home case represented partisan politics because it did not involve rational debate about alternative methods to encourage nursing homes to maintain an appropriate standard of care. Rather, the debate was accusatory and visible. The legislator was trying to force onto the agency the power to punish agency wrongdoers. According to the legislator, because the Department of Health lacked punitive powers, it did a poor job of monitoring nursing home care. In the legislator's view, to maintain quality nursing home care the Department of Health needed civil penalties in order to punish wrongdoers. Commissioner Word defined the problem differently, as "lack of appropriate care" rather than as "absence of civil penalties." In Commissioner Word's view:

> [The legislature] in January hands me a piece of legislation that gives me the authority to issue civil penalties. Then they go home in May. They would show up next January and ask if everything was all fixed. It was obvious to me that I could not allow that to happen, mainly because this agency would be committed to something that it could not deliver.

Partisan politics was being fought over the problem definition, as a Democratic legislator attempted to mobilize her party against the administration. With partisanship in play, problem definition did not emerge from a rational situation assessment; rather, the disagreement over the problem emerged in public meetings, in the legislature, and in the press. In the end, the commissioner was able to fend off the legislator's definition of the problem and to address the situation under his own problem definition. Commissioner Word, a career employee who had worked his way up the ranks over many years and had served as a middle manager in the department with several Democratic administrations, had credibility with the legislature and could be aggressive without incurring the wrath of the legislative leadership.

Commissioner Akins, Department of Personnel, an Alexander Republican loyalist, shows how sensitive commissioners usually are to the risk of offending the legislature. Akins, having defined the large number of civil service job categories as obstacles to effective administration, set about to reclassify civil service positions. He worried that reclassification would become politicized.

> The legislature was concerned that this thing was just going to be a political thing, that the Republicans would get raises and the Democrats would be left out . . . I was always scared to death that we would become a campaign issue.

The legislative branch is involved directly in defining problems—as in the nursing home situation or civil service reclassification. Commissioner McCullough in his building plan tried to use politics to leverage his proposal by mentioning a prominent former legislator. Linking his plan with this well-known Democrat communicated that this problem was responding to a need identified by the legislature earlier, thereby perhaps broadening ownership of the building plan. If the Republican administration's problem definitions were perceived as seeking political advantage, then a legislature with Democratic Party majorities in both houses could change the nature of problem identification from a focus on "what needs improving" to a focus on "who is getting what." The risk faced by a commissioner is that identifying any issue in a way that can be perceived as partisan increases the likelihood of adverse repercussions for the agency, other administration-supported legislation, and electoral politics.

The legislature and the department heads are bound together in the policy-making process through the budgetary, constituent service, and oversight processes in the legislature. When a departmental issue becomes politicized, the number of participants in the process increases, and executive control of the process diminishes. Consequently, the department executives all mentioned that they spent time talking to legislators and making sure that relations between the department and the legislature were as amicable as possible.

Discretion and Choice

With the exception of the Department of Education, where the governor had a personal interest, Alexander's cabinet members had wide discretion. Many commissioners would echo Commissioner Sansom's statement: "I just go and do what needs to be done." Identifying what needs to be done is in the eye of the beholder. A commissioner's background, skills, and previous experience influence what he or she sees as a problem or issue to be addressed. A government executive draws upon various competencies in managing a state agency: substantive competence in the policy area of the department, organizational competence in understanding and being able to maneuver in the state government bureaucracy, and sensitivity to the political environment and operating effectively in it.

Commissioners without *substantive experience* in their department's area of expertise did not identify problems having to do with the core focus of the department. For example, Bob Farris, coming from retail sales in the garment industry to the Department of Transportation, selected excessive inventory as a problem. As commissioner of F&A, Hubert McCullough had overall financial responsibility for running the government. From his expertise in building construction and facilities management, efficient space utilization assumed priority.

Having *government experience*, meaning that the executive will understand how government bureaucracy operates, shows up as a focus on internal operating efficiencies. Commissioner Olsen commented on how her experience in the Department of Revenue shaped her agenda as commissioner of personnel. "I didn't want to make the same mistake I'd made in the Department of Revenue, not doing early on what I sensed needed to be done." A lack of understanding of how government works will show up later as an implementation issue. Commissioner Simons, charged with keeping low the cost of running the government, was careful to measure cost-effectiveness on all proposed changes in her department.

An executive with *political skills* is likely to see opportunities that others would not think to look for, as with Farris and federal transportation spending (see story in chapter 4) and Donelson with University of Tennessee admission standards. Both Farris and Donelson used their extensive contacts in government to achieve goals that they favored. Donelson commented that without his extensive personal relationships with members of the legislature, the UTK standards policy would not have been possible.

The arbitrary, subjective nature of problem identification is further illustrated in the stories told by three pairs of commissioners, who headed the same departments. Akins and Olsen (personnel), Farris and Sansom (transportation), and Donelson and McCullough (F&A) told stories that described widely different department priorities.

Governor Alexander, following the advice of many governors and experts, wanted to focus on the few policies that he identified as important to his administration. In important departments of less interest to him he chose individuals who would take responsibility to manage the departments. Alexander spent considerable time in identifying talented individuals, then authorized them to set their own agendas. The large grants of discretion allowed these appointees to identify problems from their own perspectives.

Position, Perspective, and Politics at the Top of the Organization

A newly appointed cabinet member may know little about the agency's primary tasks and even less about the agency's management team, yet this executive must walk in and immediately take charge. The commissioner, as organization executive, selects the problems to be handled by the department, and the problems chosen by the commissioner can have broad impact on the citizens of the state. The devolved management system used by Governor Alexander allowed the agency executive to pursue a personally defined agenda.

The executive's perspective on departmental problems is more significant than the middle manager's perspective. Unlike the middle manager, the executive's preferences play an important part in defining a departmental mission. Previous experience, whether in the substantive area of the organization, state government operations, or the political process, is related to the executive's problem identification activities.

Partisan politics has the potential to permeate each issue that touches the executive level. Coping with policy demands made by political actors is a commissioner task. Bargaining-compromise-accommodation activities, rooted in partisan politics, impinge upon the problem identification activities of the top department executives because it is an undeniable and a legitimate element in their work environment.

Wide decision latitude does not insulate commissioners from problems bubbling up from below or coming from the external environment. These are inevitable and unpredictable. Regardless of partisan politics and personal preferences, the commissioner is heading an operating agency of government and must deal with the problems reaching that level.

CONCLUSIONS

Problem identification is a standard early step in decision process models. We commenced with this perspective, and the entry of politics into the problem definition or agenda-setting process was unsurprising. However, during the interviews with commissioners it became clear that in many situations the executives were framing their agenda based on preconceived notions drawn from their life experiences prior to joining government. This insight was reinforced by the observation that executives who succeeded each other in a specific agency had sharply differing policy priorities for the agency. It appears that an agency's problems and opportunities, and mission are not an objective reality to be discovered by careful search and analysis but constructed realities emerging from the prior history and experiences of those agency heads. Reality constructed by the governor is determinative of policy if the governor adopts a centralized administrative structure, where policy is carefully crafted in consultation among the governor and close advisors. In a centralized administrative structure, the governor's staff dominates the policy agenda. Cabinet members are more policy implementers than policy makers. Leadership ability is less important than managerial skill.

In the Alexander governance model, where the governor picks one or two priority issues and tells the rest of the cabinet to go and do good, keep the agency within budget, and avoid negative publicity, cabinet selection has important policy implications. The cabinet member will follow the issues, strategies, and management style that have brought success heretofore, upon which appointment to the high government position was based.

Middle managers operate under substantial constraints, regardless of the governor's relationship to staff and cabinet. Middle managers are bombarded with issues from above and below, and from colleagues in other units. They have a limited space within which to further a personal agenda. To achieve their goals and to be proud of these accomplishments, they must be stubborn, flexible, articulate, attentive, forthright, and passive, depending on the needs of the moment. Taking a challenging situation and turning it into a success requires astute assessment. The room for agenda setting in problem identification is less for middle managers than for commissioners.

Examining decision making has been central to organizational studies, but consensus is moving toward the view that the important consideration is agenda setting or problem identification, not the decision of what to do once a problem is identified. Every problem has a limited set of alternative solutions associated with it, but the problems themselves are unlimited. Weick (1995) shifts the focus from decision making to "meaning making" and thus looks closely at how people make sense of events in organizations, thereby identifying what is happening and what needs to be done about it. Once the problem is defined, the next step is to array the solution options and consequences and to choose among the options.

FOUR

Considering Alternatives
and Making the Decision

ONCE A PROBLEM OR AN OPPORTUNITY has been selected and identified, generating options for a solution or an action proceeds. But problem-solving behavior is difficult to detect (Scott 1979). The rational model dictates that the decision maker list alternative ways to solve the problem and attach likely consequences and probabilities to each alternative solution. Having completed this assessment, the decision maker evaluates the range of solutions and their probabilities of success against the intended goal and then selects the best alternative. The selected alternative is handed to implementers, who employ the same decision process for the implementation stage. The futility of listing alternatives and attaching probabilities is well known.

Rational choice assumes clear goals and priorities. Most public-sector organizations do not have a coherent, well-defined set of preferences. Rather, public organizations have multiple actors with asymmetric preferences, not only about the problem definition but also about how to handle the problem once it is defined. The static nature of the model raises other issues. Large organizations rarely move quickly. While the problem is being debated, time passes, new players join the discussions, the environment fluctuates, agency priorities are reevaluated, levels of participation vary, and the problem definition may change. A neat, sequential model satisfies a natural desire for order but misses the messiness present in the usual administrative decision process. The rational-comprehensive model, probably an image of the ideal in the minds of many decision makers, has been shown to be a faulty representation of what actually happens (Cohen, March, and Olsen 1972). Rational choice does not describe the administrative decision process in the stories that executives and middle managers told us.

Multiple streams analysis (Kingdon 1984; Zahariadis 1999) draws heavily upon Cohen, March, and Olsen's (1972) garbage can explanation of policy making, and closely resembles the decision process present in manager narratives. Both garbage can and multiple streams analysis assume fluid participation (the pool of decision participants changes at each meeting), problematic preferences (the preferences of the group making the decision are not stable), and unclear technology (the effective means to achieve the desired end are uncertain).

Our findings about state manager decision making are compatible with "multiple streams." Alternatives were not listed and then compared to each other but were accepted or rejected sequentially along the way to reaching a decision. With few exceptions, generating alternatives, speculating on likely consequences, and selecting among the alternatives were not separate activities but part of a process that involved many small decisions and multiple iterations, culminating in a solution that was acceptable to enough of the decision-making participants to proceed to implementation. When a solution encountered difficulties during implementation, the manager would reassess the alternatives or perhaps go back and redefine the problem. Decisions are not segmented into stages as indicated by the rational model but emerge from a process best seen holistically.

In the convoluted decision process present in the stories we heard, it was difficult to separate the alternatives assessment stage from the decision stage. Separation of stages characterizes the rational model; a confluence of stages fits "garbage can" or "multiple streams." What we heard also differs from Simon's "satisficing" and Lindblom's "incrementalism" because our decision makers did not stop the search when an agreeable solution was found; rather, they looked for a decision that would facilitate implementation. The multiple streams model best describes the decision process used by the executives and managers analyzed here.

March (1989) describes decision making as based on an interpretation of the situation. Decisions are highly contextual and surrounded by myth and ritual (Kingdon 1984; Zahariadis 1999). This contextual character injects dynamism and uncertainty into a process in which context, actors, and problems undergo change unpredictably. Reed (1991, 561) thus summarizes March:

> Decision-making preferences are often inconsistent, unstable, and externally driven; the linkages between decisions and actions are loosely coupled and interactive rather than linear; the past is notoriously unreliable as a guide to the present or the future; and . . . political and symbolic considerations play a central, perhaps overriding role in decision making.

We conclude, after reviewing the interviews many times, that the search for alternative solutions depicted in the managers' and executives' stories has more to do with getting those involved to accept and ultimately to implement the plan than it does with comprehensive analysis (rational-comprehensive model) or attempting minor changes from past policies (incrementalism).

Making the decision, when it could be separated from the search for alternatives, was determined by the ability to decide. The manager or executive who had sufficient power to decide and was comfortable with a particular decision generally acted unilaterally. Hierarchical rank plays a role in being able to move a problem quickly through the decision process. Considering the alternatives and consequences of alternative solutions and making the decision will be examined in this chapter.

CONSIDERING ALTERNATIVES AND MAKING DECISIONS: MIDDLE MANAGERS

Once the issue has been identified as a problem that should be addressed, examining alternative solutions begins. Middle managers meet with those involved in the problem and who are to be involved in the solution. At middle levels of the bureaucracy, managers cannot decide unilaterally unless the problem is technical or within the confines of their own supervisory unit. They must meet.

Density was a determining factor in the ease and the time needed to move toward a decision. Density is the extent to which competing interests and individuals are active on various sides because of this specific issue, or the structural density because of the location in the bureaucracy where the question is being addressed. Thus density includes stakeholders and clients who are active because they hope to obtain benefits or avoid losses, other departments or other units in the same agency, or even citizens. The more people legitimately and actively involved in the process, the more dense the decision-making environment. Meetings are a manifestation of density.

Assessment and Decisions: High-Density Issues

Meetings were used extensively by middle managers to generate and assess alternatives for solving the problem. Stakeholders usually were included. Assessment of alternatives proceeded slowly over time. Some obstacles were removed, other problems emerged. As time passed, issues disappeared and reappeared; participation fluctuated, proposals came and went, small steps were taken toward moving the issue forward, and perhaps a decision taken terminated the discussion.

Meetings have various purposes. Meetings to resolve problems of internal structure can also improve morale and internal group dynamics. Meetings were not only a method for determining how to create a healthier and more productive environment but were the vehicle for *getting the different members of the work unit to talk to one another.* The means for assessing what is wrong with the situation became the means for solving the problem. Successfully meeting represented a successful result.

A National Institute of Corrections team identified a problem within the Department of Correction as a dysfunctional decision environment. According to the middle manager:

> Decision making was not shared. There was no trust. There was a lot of suspicion. There was little communication, if any, with the field. Central office was viewed as the villain by most field staff and some regional directors. Just a lot of suspicion, and as they call it, the spirit of intrigue. This was three years ago. . . . This is when the consultant first started to work with us. We would get to a point that everybody would get so frustrated that they would say, "just let George do it, let him do it." They wanted me to do it again. They wanted to give up and let me make the decisions. Of course if we had done that, it [the bad environment] would have just started all over . . . I would have made the decisions, they would have said, "See, I told you; I knew that is what you would have done." He forced us, he would not let us do this. He forced this group to get back on track and make decisions. We spent two and a half months before we could even decide what the goals and objectives were. I am talking about working ten hours a day sometimes. We would come in and work ten hours a day for two or three days. The whole group. Eleven of us. We would get so frustrated and just want to pull our hair out.

The emotional drain of these meetings should not be underestimated. The middle managers who identified morale and office climate as an issue that they needed to fix would call meetings to assess which office issues were particularly troublesome and what should be done to rectify the situation. The meetings ostensibly were to assess alternative strategies, but the meetings themselves became the means to create a better work environment. The story continues:

> Once we got those goals and objectives done it was much easier. We had learned how to work with each other. Now I'll tell you, if somebody tried to take that process away from them now, they would have a real problem. . . . You go in those offices and you feel the difference in the atmosphere.

While the meetings were developing the communication, morale, trust, and confidence that characterize a positive work environment, the routine work of the managers was accumulating on their desks back in the office. Not only were middle managers forced to spend long hours with people they did not necessarily want to meet with, but their work pressures increased since their workload was not adjusted to account for many hours in meetings.

Meetings used to discuss an *externally focused substantive issue* relating to the work of the agency will include individuals from outside the middle manager's area, and if the meeting produces an agreement among those affected by the problem, then it is considered a step toward resolving the problem, but it could not be identified as part of the implementation process. Middle managers who told stories of solving a substantive problem also used meetings as their vehicle to assess alternative strategies. However, contrary to the internally focused meetings, which generally included only agency people, these meetings included many of the parties affected by the problem. Meetings to deal with a substantive problem were interactive events where the participants moved toward an acceptable decision that could be implemented. The following example involves health care policy.

> So we put the package together and went back again to the hospital people and presented an alternative plan. They didn't like it, so we went through the same process again, tried to make some more policy decisions, more alternatives, put some more incentives in there. . . . Went back to the hospital association and we still had some difficulty; so what we decided to do was to let some of the hospital people work with us, try to come up with a good alternative that we could live with. So we did that, and we worked together for another two or three months.

Meetings called and attended by mainly middle managers to solve a problem included affected parties from outside the department and in some cases outside government. Middle managers from the departments of Health and Finance & Administration, as well as private health care providers, assessed alternatives and made decisions in an interactive process. The group evolved toward a decision over time. Assessing alternatives could not be separated from deciding. A series of small decisions made by different groups over time resulted in a workable outcome, but to discriminate between the assessment and the decision is not a useful way to characterize what transpired.

Issue density may influence whether the policy-making process is composed of discrete steps or is a continuous flow. Additionally, if the issue falls into a dense structural network, then a fluid, iterative, and overlapping decision-making process is likely to emerge.

Assessment and Decisions: Low-Density Issues

There are two exceptions to the blending of assessing alternatives and decision making for middle managers, and both are low density and at opposite poles on the controversy dimension. If no controversy exists around the idea or plan of the middle manager to solve the problem, then

the superior just says, "Do it." Alternately, if the problem generates disagreement between two or more individuals or groups that cannot be
solved by accommodation or compromise, then a higher-level decision
maker steps in to decide. In both of these decision-making situations, it
may be possible to distinguish the assessment of alternatives from decision
making. In all other situations, the middle manager decision process does
not differentiate the assessment of alternatives from making the decision.
Both irresolvable disagreements about the way to solve the problem and
complete agreement about the method to solve the problem may produce a
transparent, linear decision process where considering alternatives is visibly
separate from deciding. A middle manager from the Department of Financial Institutions offers this example.

Complaints were coming into the Department of Financial Institutions
about money orders purchased by citizens in regular retail outlets being
returned for insufficient funds. The middle manager in charge began by
researching the extent of the problem and soliciting solutions in a staff meeting. The standard alternative—throw money at the problem—was obvious:
request enforcement regulations and financial support to hire personnel to
begin visiting the state's drug stores and supermarkets that offer money
orders. This obvious strategy cost money that the manager would have to find
in an already tight budget. Staff presented another strategy. A clerk called
around to other states about how they handled that regulatory responsibility.
One state monitored fines paid to the state by money order, checking to see
that all sellers were licensed. The Tennessee Department of Safety required
fines to be paid by money order. The manager recognized the beauty of this
simple solution. He called the head of the traffic fine section of the Department of Public Safety and received permission to examine those records once
a month. He then asked his boss if he agreed with this idea. The supervisor
accepted the solution. So half a day once a month, a secretary goes to the
Department of Public Safety and checks the money orders for unregistered
vendors. Having found an unregistered vendor, the manager sends a letter
detailing the fine for noncompliance. A copy of the letter goes to the bank that
has the account, telling them to freeze the account until the vendor has
obtained a license.

The assessment of alternatives and recommended decision, which
occurred at the middle manager's level, was authorized by the assistant commissioner. The problem was defined and alternatives generated in a low-density environment. The issue was low density because only one government
office had responsibility for the problem (low environment density) and stakeholders were not aroused (low issue density). The manager gathered alternative solutions from other states, came upon a solution that seemed feasible,
and recommended it to his superior, who approved it. The problem-solving
process matched the steps of the rational model.

In the case below, a budget analyst had changed the budget proposal system for the Department of Mental Health in order to allow for comparison among facilities in the field institutions. One institution within the targeted department strongly objected. The budget analyst described the meetings:

> Most of the time it goes very well. We meet, the staff works out all the issues, we have some disagreements, but we manage to hit some common ground. We usually have agreement on 95 percent of the issues. That's the way the meetings usually are. Well, I did not get agreement with the agency before we went into the meeting, could not. They just didn't agree with me. . . . I managed to sell it [the budgeting arrangement] to Lewis Donelson [commissioner of F&A]. He bought it, and that is what their budget ended up being. The agency didn't like me a whole lot, but the next year we found them more in line.

The issue was between middle managers in two government departments; no external stakeholders. The upper level of the Department of Mental Health appears not to have gotten involved, so density was low. The stark alternatives—the alternative proposed by the analyst and the alternative offered by the institution—were clear, and the differences could not be reconciled. As a result of the intense controversy, and the inability for the two sides to come to agreement, the decision was made at a higher level in the bureaucracy.

In the previous two low-density cases both the lack of controversy and intense controversy produced a clear distinction between the assessment of alternatives and the actual decision. In these cases, the alternatives' assessment was visible and resembled a rational and comprehensive search for alternative solutions. In a noncontroversial decision, a low-density network permitted the clean, visible decision. However, the criteria for making the decision were never explicit. Decision making was characterized by the use of power and authority: the middle managers could not proceed without an authorizing decision from a higher level. The deciding manager was presented with a limited range of alternatives and made the decision by considering only the alternatives presented. Controversial problem solving on low-density issues in low-density middle management environments can result in a clear distinction between the assessment of alternative solutions and the decision. The use of power is visible, for making the decision requires action by a higher management level. The less dense the issue and environment, the more visible and linear the decision-making process, which can be seen as a series of discrete steps arriving at a decision.

The Executive as Part of the Middle Manager's Meeting

A frequent middle manager strategy was to invite the next higher manager, or even the commissioner, to attend a meeting. Commissioner attendance at a meeting represents both symbolism and practical politics. An executive's time is a limited resource, and the commissioner's presence conveys a message about the significance of the meeting. Such meetings may occur at various stages in the decision process.

First, this might occur at the beginning of a search for alternatives and consequences to make managers aware that a problem has been defined and that a particular manager is taking on that responsibility. The superior's presence communicates the importance of the problem-solving activity being undertaken and legitimizes the time others may have to spend in meetings on that problem. Second, with the executive's appearance at the beginning of implementation, department managers are put on notice that implementation of this decision is a departmental priority. Third, at the completion of the project, the executive would come to announce or receive the important policy decision. Not only is the new policy publicized, but this occasion serves to praise the work of the middle manager, and hopefully praise will motivate others in the department to take initiative and to work hard.

Summary: Assessment of Alternatives and
Decision Making by Middle Managers

The ubiquitous meeting highlights important middle managers' skills. Because their power to command is limited, middle managers must communicate, negotiate, and move the group toward a decision. Middle managers in state government are embedded in a system that requires them to get permission from others before they can act. This normally high-density work environment requires frequent meetings to gain cooperation. Just picking a day and time to hold a well-attended meeting can be a scheduling nightmare. Relying on meetings precludes quick, spontaneous decision making by middle-level managers. Middle management decision processes are interactive and time consuming. Policy zealots are disadvantaged in this dense middle management environment because the delay, dialogue, and compromise would dissatisfy a purist. Policy zealots must either be at a high decision-making level or someone authorized by the highest level to carry out the decision. No policy zealots were found among the middle managers, or among the executives.

Meetings do not just address the problem of deciding what to do. Meetings also are used to ensure that the implementation of the policy, once agreed upon by those affected by the policy, is more likely to occur. Since implementation is the primary middle manager task, the middle managers who participate in making the decisions often are the same people who must implement the decision. Unsurprisingly, they are concerned with getting a decision that they can effectively administer.

CONSIDERING ALTERNATIVES AND
MAKING THE DECISION: EXECUTIVES

Generating options, assessing options, and making decisions at the commissioner level exhibited more varied patterns than at the middle levels. Among the executives interviewed, separating the search and assessment of alternatives from the decision stage generally came easily, because in the Alexander administration, the executive level internal decision environment had lower density than did middle management levels. The authority delegated by the governor to the cabinet members in departments other than education—the governor's priority—placed the commissioner in the role of ultimate decision maker in matters pertaining to the department. As the chief administrative officer of an operating department of state government, the commissioner can, in most internal matters, unilaterally choose to tackle some issues and ignore others, decide matters of internal management and policy, or delegate the option-gathering and assessment activities to middle levels of the organization. Because the internal environment is low density, commissioners can decide without needing to consult. As a consequence, some issues jump from problem identification to implementation, skipping over attention to assessing alternatives.

But a commissioner is not immune from becoming involved in high-density issues. As the main interface between the department and the rest of state government, the federal government, and citizens, the commissioner cannot routinely act alone. So when the department is facing external demands, the commissioner encounters a high-density environment.

The commissioner may choose to involve staff and middle managers in brainstorming alternative solutions or move with a self-generated solution straight to implementation. The following section describes situations where the commissioner involved subordinates in solving the problem.

Generating Alternatives: Internal Focus

Although agency policies had statewide implications and might require legislative approval, commissioners could choose their strategies for generating and assessing alternatives to solve the problem. Because the department executive is in the position to make the decisions, assessing alternatives ended when time ran out or when the commissioner was convinced of an alternative. Commissioner Akins describes the process of devising the reclassification plan for the Department of Personnel.

> Well, it basically came down to how we did salary policy. Basically, it was that Petro and Rachel would keep coming to me with options. We had about fifteen different options. What we would do if say, given this amount of

money, this is how we would spend it. And we would play with it. I would
sit at home at night and play with percentages, this and that. Give a little
here and take a little there. So through all of that we just came up with [our
final proposal]. . . . I came up with an improvement on the longevity pay. I
completely opposed the longevity pay, but I knew we were stuck with it. It
used to top out at fifteen years but I recommended that each year for five
years we raise it one year. It didn't cost that much money, $200,000 a year.
But that really turned them [employees' association] on, you see; so we were
able to slide in some other things over here. It was a good thing that Sansom was the commissioner of F&A because traditionally the personnel
commissioner and F&A commissioner didn't get along. We were the first
pair that did, to my knowledge. That really helped from the beginning. He
was supportive.

Commissioner Akins discussed a range of options with his middle managers and finally proposed an option, the centerpiece of which was longevity
pay, a practice he completely opposed but supported in order to ensure the
acceptance of the total package by the employees' association. Although meetings and discussions were held throughout the state, the selection of the legislative proposal occurred inside the department, with the commissioner having the final word. The close personal relationship between the personnel
commissioner and the F&A commissioner assured administration support for
the decision on a matter that affected the administration generally.

Jim Word, commissioner of the Department of Health, describes the
process by which he put together his plan to ensure quality care in nursing
homes.

We stayed here every night until 8 for about three months. The medical
director, Dr. Alsup, and a lawyer I have, who I think God sent him here as
best I can figure it out to help with this issue, who is a former legal services
attorney who has great rapport with advocacy groups and is a tremendous
lawyer. Mike Ingle is his name. Sherryl Midgett, who is assistant commissioner of that area. Ed Johnston, who is the director of quality assurance in
that area. . . . What I asked those people was what, in your opinion, is the
maximum that can be done by this agency under current rules and regulations, or what would you propose that would give a better quality of life to
28,000 people in nursing homes? Then I was going to make the decision of
what of those would be appropriate for the agency to do. I think we pretty
successfully did that in our legislation. We came out for everything. I mean
we didn't miss much. The only thing we came out opposing was civil penalties. The reason we opposed that was that we had a substitute. . . . You go
into a nursing home and there's 200 beds and twenty patients aren't being
taken care of. You can go home and write a ticket. You can write them a

ticket and charge them $500. Or you can do something about the twenty patients. The thing you can do about the twenty patients is put somebody in there and see if those twenty patients get care. Put them in there twenty hours a week and make the nursing home pay for it. We are going to put them [monitors] in there because you messed up. We are going to supervise taking care of them [patients] until you get back to where you were. Your penalty is we're going to make you pay for it. If it happens again we are going to take your license. We're going to try to take their license. That's the approach that we took as opposed to the civil penalties.

Commissioner Word worked through this problem with his staff and came up with the patient advocate, or ombudsman, as the most effective means for ensuring quality care for nursing home patients.

Commissioner Simons identified the organizational culture of the General Services Department as an obstacle to achieving her goal of "Great Service" for the agency. The department was operating in a "control" mode, while the commissioner wanted "service" as the agency's priority. Like the middle managers who wanted to improve the climate in their particular work unit, the executive's strategies for identifying the problem became part of implementing the solution. She held retreats for her top assistants to discuss the need to change and the alternative approaches to accomplish the change in climate. These meetings, like the meetings held by middle managers who were attempting to address similar problems of culture and climate, were both a way to develop alternatives and a way to solve the problem. And like the middle management meetings, these senior staff retreats elicited an emotional response, not just action plans.

I asked them [the senior staff] to come up with goals and then a plan that would support those goals. That was very threatening. I did not realize just how threatening that would be.

Since no one single method or approach was likely to solve this problem of changing agency culture from "control" to "service," alternative strategies were discussed and ultimately tried in the department. Strategies to make the office a more inviting place to work, to improve service to the other departments, to involve employees in departmental decision making, and to present a more helpful face to the other units of government were discussed. The analysis of alternative solutions was not aimed at finding the best solution; rather, multiple strategies were the preferred method of encouraging change. Senior members of the department participated, and the assessment process occurred in visible meetings and discussions. Decision making, implementation, and evaluation occur simultaneously. This is the convoluted, iterative decision process typical at the executive level. The commissioner had the authority to make a decision but wished to ensure that it was a right decision, thus the consultation with staff and subordinate line managers.

Commissioners do not always get to select the problems they address. Some internal problems land on the commissioner's desk after rising up through the bureaucracy. In a case mentioned previously, an assistant commissioner first made the decision to fire two department employees for handling a child abuse case unprofessionally. Controversy erupted in the external environment over the decision. Because of the need for confidentiality, the DHS could not strongly defend its actions. The publicity expanded the issue into a new problem, which the commissioner articulated as follows:

> The bottom line was that I also knew that we had to continue to work in that community. We were mandated by law to provide a full range of social services; family assistance programs, and so on. But our integrity was at stake, our ability to function as an office, that was part of what I had to salvage. [I needed to ensure that] . . . the appropriate discipline or professional action was taken in this situation, but also to ensure that we could continue to carry out our responsibilities in that community. . . . The time from the discovery to the time that it was finally concluded took probably four weeks. During that four-week period, and the four weeks were seven-day weeks, not five-day weeks, and sometimes eighteen-hour days, as all of this discussion went back and forth about what was the right thing to do in this instance. I didn't do anything else . . . I literally devoted all of my attention to this in a series of meetings. I met with experts . . . to talk to us about what would have been proper professional practice. . . . The county that this happened in was the most Republican county in west Tennessee, so it became a political issue. The county director was the former daughter-in-law of the Republican Party state chairman of some years ago; so it got all the Republican Party politicians involved who felt we were doing somebody in. . . . Nobody in town thought there was anything wrong with what had been done. The only villain in this case was DHS. . . . Of course they didn't know the details. . . . All the professional people in our department who knew about it were demanding resignations. . . . The two employees involved were driven to my office by the local member of the legislature . . . the community was up in arms because these were just great people.

In deciding what to do, the commissioner's narrative mentioned the following stakeholders:

- the caseworker and her superior who used incredibly poor judgment but without intent to harm
- the other DHS supervisors in the chain of command
- DHS social workers in the field demanding consideration for fieldworkers who make a mistake

- social workers advocating professional standards
- the local community in which both the social workers and the victim lived
- the local elected representatives
- the governor's office that had received letters from citizens
- the family of the child
- the public at large

The controversial terminations became a public controversy due to extensive press coverage. The commissioner took responsibility for deciding how to handle the situation and over an intense four-week period actively gathered information and professional opinion about what actually occurred and what should have happened.

The commissioner identified her task as "finding out where all the responsibility for the proper handling of the case should have been placed." The analysis of alternatives was contingent upon the picture that emerged of what actually happened in this situation and determining who was actually responsible for the failure to follow good social work practice. This information gathering took place in meetings. What to do with those responsible came only after determining who was responsible for the lapse.

> We went to that town and sat down in a closed courtroom with the DA, the lawyers on both sides, and our staff. The media was camped outside the door waiting to hear what was going on and surmising and interviewing people as they were coming in and going out. And I sat there and listened.

The commissioner visited the county office a couple of other times.

> I was trying to determine exactly what happened, who talked to whom, and what direction was given. . . . What became clear was that the person below the regional service supervisor was asked what to do . . . and he had not given clear direction of what she [social worker] ought to do when she had reported this to him. . . . Well I talked to him and I had never heard such gobbledygook in all my life . . . after a lot of sleepless nights and discussions and my own professional integrity being questioned.

This case that started as a simple issue inside the department evolved into a complicated, controversial problem that incorporated stakeholders outside government. This search for a solution is bundled with attempting to identify the problem, to establish responsibility. The commissioner's thought processes are bouncing between defining the problem and coming up with a solution. This interactivity among components of the decision-making process supports the assumption that reality is constructed rather than real, and it is compatible with multiple streams decision-making theory. While the analyst can see the factors that the commissioner is weighing when identifying the problem and making the decision, one could not predict which problem definition or which decision would be chosen.

The commissioner is a participant in the listing of alternatives, and the commissioner's contacts are drawn from a wide domain, likely to include sources not accessible to middle managers. Various stakeholders are talking to the executive, trying to convince or persuade. The commissioner has the power to decide, while the middle manager does not, and this differentiates alternatives assessment at the executive level from alternatives assessment at the middle level, even though the setting (meetings) is the same. The decision was made when the commissioner was convinced of the rightness of her chosen course of action.

Generating Alternatives: External Focus

Decision making involving stakeholders from outside the agency is ordinarily the executive's job, not the middle manager's job. Commissioners were responsible for policy initiatives emanating from their departments. They may have consulted and informed the governor's office of their activities, and they controlled the policy-making process. Because public policy making is rarely a completely in-house activity, the assessment of alternative plans to deal with a public problem could involve legislators, other agencies, and those interested citizens who chose to participate. Outside the confines of the department, the commissioner has no power to dictate policy. Although the setting for assessment of alternatives is the meeting, the dynamic of the meeting is not the same as for the internally focused assessment, because the power relationships are different. In arenas outside the department, the commissioner must negotiate and convince others in order to achieve policy objectives.

Transportation Commissioner Farris was searching for money to pay for bridge repairs, repairs that did not qualify for matching federal funds. At a transportation conference Farris met with the federal highway administrator.

> We played golf [at the conference] and became good friends. I explained to him that I have a problem with off-system bridges. Here's what I would like to do.

The transportation commissioner outlined the problem as he saw it, then the present procedures to handle the problem, and the proposed alternative reimbursement scheme. The federal official agreed with the commissioner's problem and the recommended solution. Farris continued:

> He goes back to Washington and I get a phone call. When he talked to his bureaucrats he discovered that this type of funding is called a soft match and it isn't permissible. He says, "Farris, I'm sorry I can't do it."

I said, "Would you object if I went up and tried to get the law changed?" He said, "No." So I did and we did.

The federal highway administrator agreed that it would be a good idea, but it was not possible because of the way the rules for matching funds were written. Enter politics. Farris had access to the federal legislative arena. Farris was an active Republican with close ties to Howard Baker, former Senate Majority leader and at the time President Ronald Reagan's Chief of Staff. Political connections likely facilitated passage of this obscure piece of legislation, which had a significant budget benefit for the Tennessee Department of Transportation. A state cabinet member has multiple sources of information and support on any policy, and a well-connected commissioner has resources unavailable to unconnected peers. These doors are closed to the middle managers.

Other commissioners told of interacting with the legislature to get their input early into the alternative assessment process, thereby increasing the chances of the policy gaining legislative acceptance. Commissioner McElrath spent several years cultivating legislative support for the administration's primary initiative—the education reform package. Although Health Commissioner Word could not win legislative approval for his bill, he succeeded in blocking an opposing bill. The commissioner of F&A worked very closely with the legislature. Lewis Donelson describes how he approached legislators:

> I just went over and talked to them a lot. I made numerous appearances before legislative committees. . . . In the beginning I got the governor's help and the support of the two speakers [Ned McWherter in the House and John Wilder in the Senate]. It wasn't support for a specific proposal, it was support that something ought to be done, and we'll work together, and everyone will have their input and say-so.

Consulting and informing the legislators and involving them in the assessment process facilitated legislative support for executive proposals. In the case of Alexander's Tennessee, the commissioners and legislators could negotiate without being constrained by the need for the governor's approval. Since both commissioners and legislative leaders are powerful, meetings at this level can move quickly, and decisions are possible with little outside involvement, which lowers decision density. Commissioners make it easier for themselves if they meet regularly with legislative leaders, listening to their concerns and exploring policy alternatives.

For major policy initiatives, public hearings are required in the assessment of alternatives. The nursing home management issue mentioned earlier was raised in the legislature. This forced agency action. The ombudsman proposal in response to the nursing home problem originated in the department and incorporated public comment. Public comments concerning alternative methods for monitoring nursing homes gave the commissioner public opinion on the issues facing nursing homes and brought forth suggestions that found their way into the rules. The public debate provided the executive with ideas about how to express the policy options so that the public could more readily interpret the oversight report.

Citizen complaints about policy also lead to an evaluation of the alternatives for conducting department business and can lead to changes in the policy. Commissioner Sansom met with citizens complaining about the construction of an interstate highway near their homes.

> So I started meeting with those people, citizens that were against the project. . . . I told the DOT people not to talk to me about the project because I didn't want to come from the straight DOT perspective and have my mind made up . . . I found out their [the citizens'] concerns, things like noise and cross streets at the same level, and then I got our people in DOT . . . to start looking for ways to architecturally design this project in addition to structurally design it. We got their complaints and addressed them one at a time, but one of their complaints was their desire not to build it, so we knew we had a difference of opinion.

The assessment of alternatives by the top executives occurs within formal public forums, in the legislature, and inside the agency. Assessing alternatives for policy that is focused outside the department finds the top executive actively involved with the legislature both to get opinion early in order to accommodate their legitimate demands but also to ease passage later on. The commissioner's involvement with the public is less direct, because the commissioner has a choice about attending the scheduled meeting, and it is appropriate for the commissioner's staff to conduct the hearings. Preferred leadership style and political connections affect a commissioner's strategy in seeking to achieve a favorable policy decision.

By-Passing Consideration of Alternatives

Some problems identified by the commissioner came complete with solutions attached. The commissioner framed the problem in such a way that a narrow range of alternative solutions naturally followed. No analysis on the part of the commissioner or his staff was apparent. The problems in this category are structured so that the solution to that problem is clear. If the University of Tennessee has standards of admission that are too low, then raise the standards. If the Department of Personnel is ineffectively organized, then reorganize. If the Department of Transportation has excess inventory, then reduce inventory. In each of these cases, the commissioner articulated the problem in such a way that only one decision was possible. However, defining a problem or an opportunity does not guarantee that stakeholders will acquiesce to the commissioner's proposal, or that implementation will be successful.

Commissioner Farris in the Department of Transportation identified a problem as excess inventory and directed a solution without any participation in the assessment of alternative ways to solve the problem.

> I brought in the people . . . and said we have ourselves an inventory problem. . . . Have you ever taught your guys to look at how much they use, how long it takes them to get it. . . . Every time you go out and go over this individual's activities at the garage go over his inventory with him. . . . I let them all know that I was going to start signing every purchase order.

In the Alexander administration, rarely was the commissioner obliged to consult others before deciding. The commissioner could define the problem and decide what to do without consultation. This lack of discussion of alternative strategies to solve a problem identified by the executive underscores the importance of the problem-definition phase, and it also shows the low-density environment of the top executive in a devolved governance system. The executive is rarely obligated to consult others in order to act. The commissioner can define the problem and decide what to do without consultation. The assessment process may be eliminated altogether if the executive simply commands subordinates to act.

DECISION MAKING

Issue density is a consideration for executives, but it does not dictate their day-to-day activities. Generally, the decision-making activities of the commissioner were invisible because commissioners had the authority and the power to decide. Stories told by the commissioners illustrate both command and consultation decision processes.

Command Decision

Department executives used both command and negotiation/persuasion to achieve their objectives. Both processes are available, and they are used in different contexts. One commissioner took office on the same day that a reorganization was being implemented. Reorganizations cannot be expected to take place without creating some unhappy employees. The commissioner dealt with the problem.

> So the day I walked in, everybody changed chairs. I had to immediately communicate to them that I was committed to that structure. I simply said,

"I am for this (re)organization. I have looked at it and in my judgment it is excellent. If you don't like it, you have trouble with me." That ended any discussion. I recognized the need for fine tuning—but I didn't want to rush into it.

Commissioner Donelson ruled that all new hiring would be put on hold for a year. He personally would sign all exceptions. Farris decreed that all purchase requests would be signed personally. Both hiring and signing purchase orders represent middle manager tasks. The fact that the commissioner did this routine work heightened the significance of the policy decision for every affected employee.

Commissioners decide when to stop searching for information. Human Services Commissioner Puett described arriving at her decision about culpability in the child abuse case. She had talked to all of those involved in the controversy, and finally after four weeks of discussions she found that "the final decision began to emerge." She indicated that she was not searching for consensus; the division of opinion about the case was intractable.

> I was confident that I made the right decision. [The case] had been mishandled not just by that counselor but all the way up the line. We had not acted appropriately, and to come down just on that counselor was grossly unfair. There had been lack of proper direction all along the line, and we needed to place that responsibility . . . the person I was hardest on was the highest-level person where knowledge stopped. That was the person who was demoted.

She indicated that she made the decision

> when I had learned everything there was to be learned about it, when it became clear in my own mind what was right. Nobody proposed this to me; nobody proposed the proper forms of discipline. I alone reached that conclusion. Some bought into it, some still think I was not being reasonable.

She determined when the decision was to be made and thereby closed the assessment of alternative issues and solutions among all those involved. At that point the discussion changed from what should be done to handle this problem to what the commissioner had decided to do about it.

Decision by Consultation

Although the executives had more control over their meeting schedule than did middle managers, they could not avoid meetings. When a decision needed the cooperation or consent of others, meetings were the forum. Executives' meetings differed from middle managers' meetings in that the executives had more opportunity to structure the meetings to suit their policy preferences or their managerial styles. Further, the executives, by virtue of their hierarchical position, had access to top executives in other bureaucracies, thereby short-cutting decision processes that would normally involve mid-level discussions between agencies or stakeholders, and a consensus document slowly working its way to the top.

Commissioners will often pay a call to individual legislators early in the legislative term. Consulting and informing the legislature, actively involving it in the assessment process, generates legislative goodwill, thereby laying the groundwork for cooperative relations. Commissioners and legislators can negotiate without being constrained by the need for any other approvals on the outcome of their discussions. When Darrell Akins, commissioner of personnel, was attempting to update the classification system, a legislator objected to a particular title given to a position in the new classification system. Akins changed the title. He commented, "A good relationship with the legislature is critical, and it just wasn't worth a fight." Middle managers are not usually authorized to negotiate with legislators, and even direct communication between middle managers and the legislators is circumscribed.

Because of the structure of the executive branch in Tennessee, the commissioner of F&A works closely and continuously with the legislature. Donelson illustrated the relationship between the executive branch and the legislature by indicating that he frequently walked over to see legislators, whereas executive department members walked over to see him. Consultation and accommodation are used with the legislature; command is inappropriate.

Education was a priority of the Alexander administration, so the decision-making process, which necessarily included the legislature, was carefully orchestrated. The teachers' union was uncomfortable with the merit pay provisions in the administration plan, so a group to counter the union's objections was formed, headed by the governor's mother and the son of a former Democratic governor. The commissioner of the Department of Education was a liaison to the legislature. Public opinion polls were used to demonstrate support for the program. The legislature was the forum for the decision, and the discussion issues were structured as much as possible by the administration. In this case, Commissioner McElrath was a member of the team of decision makers, with the governor and his staff acting as team leaders.

Another feature distinguishing public-sector from private-sector decision making is the extended process. Public-sector executives, on the whole, need to consult more people for clearance than executives in the private sector. Every public decision is subject to public scrutiny and multiple interpretations. As Commissioner McCullough said:

One big difference between the public and private sectors is the time required for the process. This whole thing [getting the building plan approved] is a process, and we've been working on it for a couple of years. If it were my business and I was going to develop [the plan for building state offices], I'd have been going on it a long time ago. But you go through that process, educating and getting people to buy into the program.

The opportunities for command often are present for the commissioner and infrequent for the middle managers, but the norm is consultation for both middle managers and executives, even in a devolved management system.

CONCLUSIONS

Once the problem has been identified, environment density and issue density are the key factors explaining the time spent in the decision process. Environment density is a fact of life for middle managers by virtue of their hierarchical placement; a dense environment was less often an obstacle for the executives. Issue density, the amount of activity surrounding a particular issue, controls the speed of the process and the ability to separate assessment of alternatives from the actual decision. Low-density issues provide the observer with a more transparent process.

Middle managers face downward, upward, and sideways to do their jobs. They encounter multiple interests and have overlapping responsibilities. Dense issues and environments, which demand a steady diet of meetings with peers and outsiders, are a fact of life for them. Assessment of the alternatives at the middle level occurred primarily at meetings of peers. The dense working environment of middle managers requires that they obtain cooperation, or at least acquiescence, to carry out their job responsibilities effectively.

Governor Alexander charged his cabinet to determine the agendas for their departments and granted them authority to act on these agendas. By virtue of their hierarchical position, the internal decision environment for executives was less dense than the middle managers' decision environment. Executives operating in a devolved system have the ability to decide without the consultation requirement that the middles usually face. The meetings are different and do not dominate the policy-making process at the executive level as they do at the middle manager level.

The assessment of alternatives and the decision about what to do are not naturally discrete decision stages. Assessing alternatives and coming to a decision often are mingled, making it difficult for the outside observer to discern a separation between these two stages. The rational-comprehensive model requires conscious calculations of alternatives; it neglects the intuitive decision maker whose calculations are not conscious and explicit. The rational decision model also underplays the importance of the group meetings that characterize assessment of alternatives and decision-making processes, not only at the middle level, where group meetings dominate, but also at the executive level. The conventional assumption that rationality is the overriding organizing frame misses the fact that people make plans and decisions based on friendship or animosity, gratitude or revenge, personal career goals, reputation, past personal interactions, protection of organizational base or personnel, and just plain hunches about the future. The emotional context of alternatives assessment and decision making is an important factor to consider when studying the decision process. Reality is constructed, and this construction simultaneously involves multiple stages of the decision process. The intent of a manager's actions may have less to do with the rational analysis of a situation than with the manager's feelings about the situation.

Having considered the alternatives and made the decision, the next step is implementation.

FIVE

Implementation

ACCORDING TO THE DECISION MODEL, implementation follows decision. Successful implementation of most decisions requires someone's active intervention. With a new plan or policy, some people in the organization will have to do things differently. For most people, doing things differently is resisted; most of us prefer the usual way. The familiar is comfortable, easier, and requires less mental effort, so handing a new plan to an old organization, without an intrusive intervention, will not likely achieve the desired result.

Implementation can fail if a decision maker underestimates the obstacles to effective implementation, overlooks the perspectives of employees carrying out the implementation, or ignores the opinions of stakeholders affected by the change. Resistance should be anticipated as the likely response toward any new policy, and the greater the distance between decision and implementation—whether measured by miles, administrative layers, or time—the greater the implementation challenge. Subordinates can undermine a directive from a superior by working slowly, by performing poorly in that aspect of their job, or encouraging resistant behavior by coworkers. Since the average tenure of a commissioner is less than three years, disliked policies can be drawn out until the commissioner leaves.

Our interviews reinforced the commonly held understanding that the principal task of a middle level manager is to administer, to implement. The middle manager may not have authority over others involved in the implementation, but even with formal authority, effective manager behaviors involve less commanding and more communicating, negotiating, and motivating as managers carry out the policies, decisions, or tasks handed to them by their administrative superiors. Middle managers interact daily with subordinates, supervisors, peers, clients, and constituents; and employ negotiation and communication skills (Kraut et al. 1989). Implementing decisions in situations where they lack formal control is common and tests a middle manager's credibility and communication skills.

The stories told by the executives contradicted what is generally believed about the executive's involvement in the implementation process. Although the implementation literature does not usually differentiate by management level, the operative assumption is that the executive decides, then hands the implementation task to the staff or to line middle managers. We found that executives thought seriously about the likelihood and ease of implementation as part of their decision considerations.

As described in the previous chapter, executive decisions generally took place in a less dense environment, where command was a feasible option. Simply because of their placement at the top of the hierarchy, commissioners were able to implement policy without the constraints that the middle managers faced. However, the executives' implementation rationale and behavior differ significantly from that of middle managers. Executives got actively involved in implementation because of a crisis of time or publicity, a desire to emphasize a policy decision, and when their involvement would provide major relief to middle management. Conversely, they may decline to become involved in even a major policy in order to encourage middle managers to assume responsibility for the long-term survival of the policy.

MIDDLE MANAGER IMPLEMENTATION

Middle managers are responsible for a wide range of policy implementation tasks, but they do not have a free hand to act as they wish; they are bound by rules, organizational norms, and personal relationships. Generally, public-sector rules favor equity over efficiency. Fairness is more important than speed. Mandated procedures and extensive clearances that regulate the operations of government bureaucracy require documentation to ensure that citizens receive their entitlements. Implementing even simple policies emphasizes procedures to enable stakeholders to have a hearing. Managers cannot handle a citizen's request their way, or the client's preferred way; they have to handle it in a certain, prescribed way. Rules mean that a process will likely be followed, and that process may not be speedy or efficient. Such rules, often spoken of disparagingly as "red tape," are designed to ensure consistency, predictability, and equal treatment. Organizational norms and personal relationships also affect implementation and may ease or impede the implementation of a decision.

The following represent typical middle manager implementation activities:

- A Department of Personnel manager sends 40,000 letters to present and potential state workers concerning a redesign of the classification system.

- A manager designs forms, writes the organization manuals, and creates the procedures to facilitate the operations of a financial administration system for a new project.
- A manager writes personal development plans, waiver applications, funding requests, and Medicaid and Social Security applications to state and federal oversight agencies to fund and certify a group home for elderly mentally retarded individuals.
- A middle manager designs a system to implement federal administrative directives and decisions by the state legislature.

In some situations middle managers have the authority to mandate the implementation strategy, while in other situations they lack control over the implementation process. Each implementation environment will be described in the pages that follow.

Implementing with Control

Implementing with control does not mean automatic, effective implementation. With authority, one can command, and according to the principle of hierarchy, those below should obey and implement. Two obstacles may be present to obstruct the middle manager's way. First, the implementer may not understand how to do what is required—he or she lacks knowledge. Second, even if the implementer knows what to do, he or she may not wish to carry out the directive—he or she lacks motivation. A subordinate who does not wish to carry out the middle manager's directive has a variety of ways to impede or halt the implementation process. The examples that follow illustrate each type of obstacle.

Lacking knowledge. When a high-performing employee is promoted from technician to supervisor, management anticipates improved productivity in the unit. Sometimes these expectations are fulfilled. However, supervisory skills differ from technical skills, and the employee may be incapable of implementing effectively in the new role—not for a lack of motivation but from a lack of ability. A possible answer is training; however, just as some people appear to have mental or emotional blocks against learning mathematics or foreign languages, some people appear to have difficulty learning to manage.

Two stories illustrate failures where supervisors want to do a good job, but they lack practice knowledge. They just cannot figure out how to be effective.

> After about a year we started to recognize that this man was having a lot of problems, he didn't communicate well with his employees at all. We worked with him and counseled him and did everything that we knew to do, sent him to school and had different ones go up and work with him, but the bottom

line was that this fellow, who has twenty-one years of experience, has a master's degree, has performed very well as an auditor, cannot perform as the supervisor, and we're now in the process of going through the painful process of figuring out what we're gonna do with him. We know if we put him back as an auditor, that's degrading, puts him in a horrible position. He's lived in Knoxville all of his life, and yet he can't function as a supervisor. At this point I've decided we can't remake him, it's not his skills that are the problem, it's his basic ability to deal with people. He likes to go off and just kind of be alone.

Another story:

I had a really good technical person, and she was a hard worker. Everybody liked her, so we promoted her and it just hasn't worked out. She hasn't been able to supervise people, she can't let go of the work. . . . The people who work for her don't grow because she won't turn loose. We've tried all kinds of supervisory training, performance evaluation, just everything that we know to try to keep her as a supervisor, and it's just not working. About three or four weeks ago I said, "OK, you know you really need to go on vacation." She is the type of person who will make herself sick because she'll work every night till after 12 o'clock, and is the first one in the office in the morning, works weekends, it's really hard to deal with a person like that . . . what do you do with a person who works that hard and tries so hard, a good technical person, but won't turn loose and let her people go?

Here are competent technicians, promoted to supervisory positions, who cannot manage effectively. Implementation fails if one is willing but cannot perform one's job. Dealing with an incompetent supervisor situation is the middle manager's job, and the effective manager must address that challenging, emotionally painful predicament.

Lacking motivation. If the employee knows how to do the job, or is trained within a reasonable time to carry out the responsibilities, then the performance challenge facing the middle manager is to motivate that employee. Some public employees have become comfortable carrying out their tasks in a particular way, have job security, and do not want to adjust their established routines. Job security affords government employees protection from retribution by newly elected or newly appointed political leaders. A government employee secure in the job presumably will be fair, will apply the same rules or process to every client or applicant. But for some employees this job security also brings resistance to new ways of implementing.

Punishment or threats may prevent negative actions, but are not effective at inducing high performance. Experienced employees can figure many ways to avoid both work and punishment. Alfie Kohn (1993) articulates the view that threats and extrinsic incentives can have a short-term positive effect, which wears off, leaving cynicism in its wake. Communicating the intrinsic value of high performance, convincing the employees—and generating the internal motivation to maintain a high performance level—requires the manager to commit substantial amounts of time and energy to understanding subordinates in order to gain their trust and to inspire to peak performance.

Motivational challenges faced a middle manager at a mental health facility. As residential mental health facilities lose patients, their budgets decline, and staffing levels must be reduced. Getting appropriate coverage in order to maintain accreditation means that managers and employees must devise alternative ways to meet these challenges.

Green Valley is the kind of a place where there's very little turnover, particularly in key management and program positions. Somebody gets into a job assignment and they feel that that's all there is in the world, they get tunnel vision and they think that the second shift at Alder Cottage serves all the people in the world. Of course, they're only 1/16th of what's at Green Valley; so my plan was . . . to convince particularly my management programming people that they needed to move systematically about every two to three years to a very similar job, not a different job, not the usual job cross-training kind of thing, but a programming person at one cottage would swap places with a programming person or another management person, and then after that got started even the direct care staff would begin to trade places in various places and therefore over time, in say ten years, the average employee at Green Valley in residential services would have a feel for the service delivery probably in half a dozen locations. Since our residents are so diverse, we serve residents from six months of age to ninety years of age, from mildly retarded to profoundly retarded, multiply handicapped, etc., that they would gain a wide range of competency dealing with folks and wouldn't be near as limited in their abilities to work in other places.

The real benefit that I felt to the individual (all these other things I have been talking about I can see benefit the organization because they'd be more competent within their jobs), I felt that it would keep them from being burned out, that it would be new challenges periodically and would keep the person learning and moving, and that would have some payoff individually because figuring the tenure of the average employee at Green Valley is more than ten years; so I really believe we do have folks that get to the point that they just can't come up with anything new any more, and they don't want to hear anything new . . . I tried my best to sell it to my management folk . . . they just didn't want to do it, said they would do it if I made them do it. They didn't think it had any merit, they were quite happy with what they were doing, and they really were doing a good job of what they were doing. I haven't yet gotten myself to the point that I want to disrupt the organization by forcing their choice. It's not a complete failure, because I think that probably some of the reorganization that we may have to go through within what's going on right now will give me the opportunity to make some moves that people would understand. I think that I should have been more assertive in going and getting it done. I just wasn't able to weigh the cost and benefits, and see that the hassle was worth the possible benefits.

This mental health manager faced passive resistance to his proposal. His managers were performing effectively, but they lacked the creativity and energy that may be required for the turbulent times ahead as the downsizing of residential mental health services takes place. To have mandated the shift would have created headaches for the manager on top of an already full plate. His employees were capable—they could do the job—but unwilling, and dictating a forced change would have required substantial amounts of the manager's time to motivate supervisors and frontline employees to high performance. The middle manager did not feel he had the time and energy to undertake that task at present; therefore, no action was taken.

Implementing policy, even if the manager has the ability to control his or her environment, still involves obstacles. These obstacles also apply to both middle managers and executives. All employees have to be willing and able to perform their jobs. If not, then this is a managerial time bomb and a drag on attempting to achieve long-term organizational effectiveness.

Implementing without Control

Middle managers frequently are charged with implementing in situations they do not control. Politicking does not end when an authoritative decision is made. In implementing policies enacted by the legislature or decreed by the agency executives, the struggle for control of resources and the contest to achieve a particular outcome continue after the policy is handed to the implementation agents. Managers and executives cannot hide from individuals and groups who lost the battle in the legislative arena. Interested individuals or groups continue to lobby both legislators and high-level administrators for their preferred outcomes. Citizens perceive that they have a legitimate say in ensuring that administrators do their jobs correctly.[1] And the public *should* have a voice in policy implementation, because participation in the body politic is a democratic right that cannot be abridged. Due process and citizens' rights, leading to participation by anyone interested, contribute to the high density of the middle manager's job.

Command, although sometimes available to middle managers, is not usual. More commonly, middle managers must negotiate, persuade, and generally convince others to participate. Overlapping or conflicting mandates bring on turf issues between agencies. The multiple inspections of food products in restaurants and grocery stores by the Department of Health and the Department of Agriculture, mentioned previously, illustrate that situation. Each department has its view on the best way to ensure that Tennesseans purchase only pure food. The differing perspectives of the two departments complicated implementation of the policy and further contributed to the difficulty of implementing in a dense environment.

In another example, the Department of Labor (DOL), after having decided to contract with a private advertising agency to market its Job Training and Partnership Act program, had to overcome resistance at the implementation phase from the comptroller's office.

> . . . we [DOL] ended up having to redo the RFP [request for proposal] to satisfy the comptroller's office and resubmit it and extend our time frame for getting it in. Eventually the proposals came in, and we set up a review committee. There were four on the committee, and we reviewed about thirteen proposals that came in. I had to set up a plan for reviewing so that it was an objective-type way of measuring each one. It took a lot of negotiating within the committee; it took negotiations with the commissioner. We finally got the top three firms that we settled on, and the comptroller got involved again! And so it was a constant thing of having to overdo justification of the marketing program to the comptroller. It really came down to a struggle. It took us about six or seven months to finally get a contract with an ad agency outside of state government.

The Department of Labor was focused on fulfilling its mission, while the comptroller's office was concerned with following the rules, with determining whether this expenditure was needed, and with ascertaining whether the marketing task could have been performed by a state agency rather than by contracting with the private sector. The comptroller's office was seemingly more concerned with equity and procedure than with efficiency and effectiveness. Political turf issues also are at play here. The Department of Labor is an executive agency; the comptroller's office reports to the legislature.

Middle managers strive to create relationships with stakeholders and peers outside the work group. Building these relationships is necessary because the density of the middle management environment may require authorization from those outside the work unit, over whom the middle manager has no authority. In dealing outside one's agency or up one's own hierarchy, differences in perspective, differences in importance assigned to the issues in conflict, protection of turf, or just plain contrariness can slow or stymie middle manager implementation of an agency decision. Implementing without control poses a significant challenge for the middle manager.

Talking: The primary middle manager implementation tool. Kikoski (1993) reports that managers spend 75 percent of their time communicating, reinforcing

Mintzberg's (1973) research showing that managerial activities are characterized by brevity, variety, and fragmentation. In implementing, middle managers talk a lot. They talk to convince, cajole, and direct subordinates. They talk across divisions or departments, to people over whom they have no authority, as they coordinate and negotiate peer participation in projects. They talk "up" as they reassure superiors that projects are meeting the deadlines, and they seek clearance for project changes. They talk to sell projects or programs to those whose support is necessary to implementation. They talk to ensure that goals, activities, and deadlines are clear and understood. Effective verbal communication is essential for a middle manager. Tightly fitted into a dense environment of coworkers, superiors, subordinates, and stakeholders, middle managers cannot operate without communicating extensively with interested and affected parties. Talking constitutes a large part of their day. If the middle manager cannot communicate effectively orally, then she or he cannot do the job. Talking is the foundation for the middle manager behaviors of confronting, comforting and reassuring, networking, and team building (Kanter 1989). Deciding which combination of specifics in confronting, comforting, or reassuring is likely to be effective in generating the appropriate results in a particular situation tests the manager's practice knowledge daily.

Talking may not sound like implementation, but it is the key to getting others to cooperate and perform. Talking is not just one thing; it takes numerous shapes. We illustrate next the kinds of talking used by middle managers in getting their colleagues and subordinates to perform at a high level of competence.[2]

Confronting. The manager of the patient advocacy unit implementing Commissioner Word's directive on protecting the rights of nursing home residents had been unsuccessful in several attempts at eliciting the appropriate level of commitment from her subordinate. She called in the subordinate and was prepared to give her a written warning.

> I said, ". . . let me tell you what I have got on my mind, and if you need to take some notes with what I am saying, please do, but I don't want to be interrupted. You will have a chance to defend every point that I am making, or to make comments." . . . We went over the points. It worked quite well. We developed a dialogue with each other, an understanding. Some things that she came back to me with: "You are too serious, or at least you appear to be too serious when you talk about things." . . . We have built since then a very good relationship. . . . We still have a lot of growth yet to go with each other. I think we are headed in the right direction. . . . We had an opportunity to travel to Knoxville on some complaints together. . . . She looked me square in the eye and said, "You are the first person that has ever dealt with me in a very direct manner and said to me what you don't like and what you do like and what your expectations are. And because of that I respect you.

You scared the hell out of me. I thought, 'Boy, I am gone. This is it.' But the more you talked, the more I saw I had an opportunity to do the job well. Which is what I want to do."

This confrontation changed the attitude and behavior of the employee, and a positive working relationship resulted.

Confronting works best in tandem with accommodating. The F&A middle manager responsible for the Department of Mental Health made a decision that many of the institutions under his charge found extremely annoying, ("the agencies didn't like me a whole lot"). To smooth out the relationships he went out to visit every facility to talk to the managers, talked to them about the parts of his decision that they "had real heartburn about," and made small adjustments when the mental health agency could justify its request. His rationale for visiting was that he had to be able to work with them in the future and he had to establish that he was a reasonable person who could be trusted. Trust develops more easily if engagement accompanies confrontation (Cunningham 1989).

Comforting and reassuring. According to Ryan and Oestreich (1998), fear in organizations makes managers act to evade threat. Fear destroys trust, erodes joy, stifles innovation, and distorts communication (Briskin 1996; Kouzes and Posner 1988). Comforting and reassuring subordinates was present in many of the middle managers' stories. Some managers used retreats or large non-work-related gatherings so the employees could get to know one another to reassure themselves that others in the larger organization were not antipathetic toward them or unconcerned about their interests and duties. One manager used not only retreats to address an uncomfortable working environment, she also used other gatherings.

Christmas parties, special holidays, on birthdays we have cake and ice cream. Just little things. I feel like if you take care of the little things then the bigger things take care of themselves. If you address them, show them that you care and make a special effort to go the extra mile, then productivity goes up. The atmosphere seems a lot better. It is working. We're not perfect yet, but it's working.

Other middle managers sought to create a comfortable work environment by setting clear standards, measuring accomplishments, and using positive reinforcement. A manager left his office a couple of times during the year to work beside his frontline employees. By cooking in the prison kitchen, or doing another line job, the middle manager felt that he would better understand subordinates' perspectives, and that the bonds would be strengthened between him and his colleagues, that morale would be maintained, and that implementing would not be obstructed by personal issues.

Allowing and encouraging the participation of subordinates in decision-making processes was another technique for comforting and reassuring. A middle manager who used group decision making indicated:

> We all have the same amount of power. We share in the power. We really feel like it has done more [than any other technique] to improve the health of our organization.

Networking, using personal contacts. Using personal contacts to ease a program through trouble spots was a common implementation practice. The Department of Agriculture is responsible for pest control. A federally funded survey of East Tennessee found a large concentration of gypsy moths in Johnson County, a locale close to Maryville, the home of the governor. The governor had expressed interest in the problem. The Department of Agriculture requested funds for spraying, and these funds were budgeted but not available until July, the beginning of the new budget cycle. However, the moths would not wait until the beginning of the budget cycle; the spraying needed to be done in April. The commissioner responded by saying, " Go ahead and do the spraying, we'll find the money." At this point, the commissioner dropped out of the process; finding the money to pay for the program fell to the middle manager.

When the middle manager approached his F&A department counterpart with the problem, *"The F&A guy says, 'Hey, there's a lot of problems out there, every department has a problem.'"* This Department of Agriculture middle manager had to spend considerable time assembling the money. He transferred money from accounts in the department, and some departmental employees had to wait several months for their travel expenses to be reimbursed.

> A lot of times he [the commissioner] doesn't realize the impact on the actual work program, the day-to-day operations. . . . [The cost of spraying] had serious impact, we had employees who couldn't get travel checks. . . . It could have been handled a lot more easily, a lot cleaner, had the commissioner gone in and said, "Hey, we've got a problem, we've got to spray next month, and we need to get something done" [to move money into that department]. Certain levels I could go to and that's it, that's when the commissioner needs to get involved.

The middle manager was able to accomplish the task but at the cost of ill will from employees who had to wait until the new fiscal year to receive their travel reimbursements. Being in the middle of the organization limits a manager's reach. Middle managers cannot focus attention and gain the ear of another department as easily as their commissioner can.

Team building. When ineffective implementation results from a poorly performing group of employees, some managers pursue team building to improve the prospect of successful implementation. Resulting from the commissioner's directive, two units from the Department of Human Services were merged and shoved into cramped quarters. No one was pleased about this change, and employees from the units were not cooperating, or even being civil to one another. The middle manager in charge was now supervising those who formerly supervised her.

What I started doing was spending time with them, wandering around talking to them, getting to know their job, not to say, " I'm here to dictate to you," but to say, "I want to learn what you're doing, how you are doing it. If I have any suggestion to offer you, I'll do that, but I'm not here to change what you're doing. I just want you to know I'm not a threat, not coming in and making a lot of changes." The first thing I wanted to do was to have some time for ourselves, get away from the offices, spend some time getting to know each other, and saying, "These new people are ok, they're not a threat to you; they're not going to take over your job. They have jobs themselves." . . . We went off to a three-day retreat and we really got some real feelings on the table and dealt with those. When we left there I felt good that we were feeling good about ourselves and we had started that trust building. We were able to start planning some things for the unit, little things, having once-a-month things like a salad bar or a taco bar or breakfast, come in and sit down and just have some socialization. We were not doing that; they were just very isolated and would not talk to each other. I was trying to get communication going and start developing some relationships.

The next time we started talking about real feelings, about why . . . that person has twenty-two contracts and I have fifty contracts. "I feel like I do more work than they do, we should be at the same level." It was competition between positions, some jealousy going on, and we wanted to talk about those things. . . . We just came back from a staff retreat last week. This time we brought in contract audit. [We] felt like we needed to start internally doing some networking because we work with those people on a day-to-day basis, we work side by side, felt like there was a need, now that we have our unit on the right track and feel good about it, then let's start working with other units. So I feel good where we are, looking at where we were a year ago to where we are now. We've accomplished a lot, and I think a lot of that has to do with the fact that I showed them that I cared, did little things for them, got other supervisors involved with them, and paid attention to their problems, just listening to them.

This middle manager saw that her unit could not implement effectively until internal relationships between her and employees, and among employees themselves, were repaired. She worked on the two tracks simultaneously. Team building by employing an outside consultant addressed inter-employee relationships; her extensive involvement in these sessions demonstrated personal concern for the welfare of each employee and over time engendered trust between employees and supervisor. Later, seeking to reduce fears about the external unit that monitored their work, she brought in peers from outside the unit to explain their perspective.

Middle Manager Implementation: Summary

In implementing policy middle managers spend their work days on the phone, completing reports, writing manuals, coordinating efforts, negotiating cooperation, selling strategies, visiting field offices and job sites, filling in forms, designing forms, preparing demonstration projects, and talking, talking, talking. They meet with others involved in the implementation, and they include in their discussions those stakeholders likely to impede the project. Involving others and attempting to build trust is not co-optation.[3] The outside agencies and groups are not seduced to accept the middle manager's plan; rather, the typical implementation is iterative and inclusive so that those who could stop the middle manager from successfully pursuing the implementation of a policy are accommodated in the process. The middle manager gains information regarding the nature, intensity, and rationale for objections by subordinates so she or he does not waste time considering a useless implementation strategy. Personal contacts with peers facilitate implementation; inviting or cajoling the commissioner into appearing at department functions emphasizes the importance of a project.

The implementation process at middle management levels often operates in a dense environment of individuals and groups who have varying levels of investment and power in implementation decisions. Dense environments require extensive meetings and contact with those concerned and those who may be able to hinder the implementation effort. Implementation through situations of high density requires meetings. Middle management generally involves small- and medium-size groups that meet to decide, negotiate, accommodate, diffuse conflict, gather information, and smooth out the obstacles impeding policy implementation, as well as policy decision.

Public-sector middle managers do necessary, often unglamorous, work. In the private sector, when an authoritative decision is made, the organization is expected to put forth a concerted effort to accomplish that goal. In the public sector, where efficiency subordinates to procedures, stakeholders to the issue get another bite of the apple. What one group loses at the decision stage may be reclaimed at the implementation stage. Edelman (1964) has documented this in his discussion of symbolic and instrumental rewards, and Schattschneider (1960) has shown that interests that lose in one arena shift to another arena in order to turn the decision in their favor.

Srivastava et al. (1994) have shown middle managers to have higher anxiety and stress levels than either executives or workers. This is not surprising. Meetings make for just as slow and frustrating of a decision-making process at the implementation stage as at the decision stage. But meetings also make for acceptable, implementable, and sound decisions and serve to build trusting relationships among participants.

EXECUTIVE IMPLEMENTATION

Unlike middle managers, whose primary work is implementing policies and programs, executives, in theory, spend their time visioning the future, defending the agency's resources against "predators," seeking beneficial collaborations, defining problems and opportunities, and making decisions. Cabinet members *did* emphasize these activities. However, executive effort also went into implementing in those difficult situations that an organization head can accomplish more easily and effectively than a middle manager. First, executives may implement systemic policy changes that subordinates do not like. The executive, by virtue of positional authority, can carry out the action without challenge. Subordinates may not like it, but they cannot challenge it.

Second, high-profile issues in the external environment that affect the agency are best handled by the executive. Stakeholders from within or without may obstruct the work of a middle manager but are more likely to acquiesce to the request of the commissioner.

Third, the executive can secure diffuse emotional support and legitimacy for the agency's agenda. The commissioner is the leader of the agency, sets the tone for the agency, and has prestige both inside and outside. Employees at all levels appreciate attention from the leader. Paying attention to rank-and-file employees boosts morale and enhances support for the executive's articulated goals.

Additionally, because the executive has the discretion to participate or not participate in the implementation of a policy or program, it is interesting to examine when the executive is absent from the process. Having identified a program as important to the success of the commissioner's tenure, the same commissioner may refuse to become involved in the implementation of the program, preferring to assign the task to a deputy. The issue is ownership. A commissioner will likely remain in office fewer than three years.[4] If the commissioner is pushing the program, then it may languish or die when the commissioner leaves; if an assistant commissioner is in charge and takes ownership of the program, then the program has a better chance of continuing past the departure of the original champion.

Arbitrary, Tough, Systemic Decisions

Finance Commissioner Lewis Donelson threatened the other cabinet members that if they could not commit to a staff reduction and follow through with that promise, then he himself would make the personnel decisions.

We would have those unfortunate meetings in which they would say, "We can't do this," and we'd say, "Well, you'd better get used to it because you're gonna have to." It was amazing how many times I would say what we're gonna have to do, and they would say, "Totally impossible," and I'd say, "Well, go back and try harder," and they would come back and say, "We worked it out, we can do it." It emphasized the fact that they didn't really, they hadn't given it as much real organizational thought as they could. I think that worked out very well. I don't think there was a great deal of trauma. I mean there was trauma initially with some of the commissioners and when I said, "You're gonna have to do this, we'll allow you to shift those [positions] any way you want to, and yet reduce them." It required constant pressure. . . . We passed the rule that no new person could be hired without my personal approval for a year. It was a hell of a lot of work, awful lot of work, but we actually went for a year in which every request for a new employee, not transfers or anything like that, but the hiring of a new person, even though you had a vacancy, to fill that vacancy it had to come to my office to be approved. I think that worked very well. I don't think it really created trauma in the department. We did virtually no firing. We did some fairly arbitrary transferring.

Commissioner of Transportation Bob Farris told of finding millions of dollars in inventory stored in warehouses throughout the state. The commissioner diagnosed the problem as lack of incentives for the warehouseman to limit his supplies. The warehouse employee could get in trouble with a supervisor if he did not have the item—there was no penalty for having too much inventory. The warehouse employee was acting rationally from a personal perspective by keeping the storehouse full of parts and equipment, however it was not rational for the organization because millions of dollars that could have been used for roads and bridges were sitting on warehouse shelves. The commissioner highlighted his emphasis on cutting inventory by adopting the strategy previously used by Donelson, personally signing every purchase order.

I let them all know that I was going to start signing every purchase order. . . . So I take the time, sometimes on Saturday mornings, sometimes after hours, and I look at every purchase order. . . . The first year we took a million dollars off the inventory. That million dollars went right out into road projects instead of sitting on shelves gathering dust.

We questioned the executive's use of time—it is contrary to organizational management teachings to have the top executive micromanaging the department by signing requests for oil filters and pencils. Commissioner Farris defended his action by stating that if he had delegated the implementation of inventory control, then the bureaucracy would shift into gear. There would be meetings, decisions about appropriate levels of inventory, discussions of regional variations, forms to design and copy, job descriptions adjusted to include new activities—all the things that organizations do in order to get control of resource expenditure. The commissioner had circumvented tens of hours of meetings and paperwork. At the same time he had ordered a new inventory and purchasing system to be installed in the department within the next three years. So he spent a few hours each week and saved the department's middle management hours of meetings and deliberations. He immediately stopped the financial hemorrhaging and took steps to solve the problem in the long term by initiating a computerized inventory management system.

These aggressive, arbitrary, hands-on actions by the executive communicated the intensity of the executive's commitment to the policy. The executive took the policy seriously: everyone else must get on board or be in open opposition to the commissioner. There was no time for trickle down, for gradual accommodation for unique circumstances. If there were exceptions, they would be few, and they would come from the top.

The commissioner's likely short tenure means that priorities must be accomplished immediately to avoid getting bogged down with process. High visibility communicates effectively to those lower in the organization who may put little stock in written words and documents. No middle manager exhibited an aggressive, directive, or threatening implementation style. A middle manager cannot unilaterally hire, fire, or halt purchase orders. These tools can be wielded only by the commissioner.

Public Visibility

When a departmental issue or action becomes controversial and the public eye is focused on the department, the department executive may play a role in implementation as well as decision making. Commissioner Puett of Human Services found herself caught in a controversy that involved accusations of child sexual abuse, a vocal local community and politicians, a major split in her own department about how to handle the situation, citizen calls to the governor's office, extensive newspaper coverage, and strong professional opinions within her close staff to fire longtime employees. There was no keeping a low profile when deciding what to do about this problem, nor was there pressure from the governor as to how the matter should be resolved. It was an agency decision, and Commissioner Puett was in charge. In announcing and implementing the decision,

> I flew to the county to meet individually with each of the people involved with the case and give them the decision face-to-face, not delegated from the commissioner to counselor to supervisor to county director. Of course, everybody was in the county office. If looks could kill I would have been dead the

minute I set foot in the door. I am surprised that they didn't shoot down the
plane. Nobody knew what the decision was until they heard it from me,
nobody knew that.

The commissioner indicated that the department still had to work in
the county where the controversy erupted, and she needed the respect of her
staff to continue to direct the agency, and these two stakeholders held opposite opinions on the case. The high visibility of the situation, the extensive
press coverage, and the active participation of elected politicians forced the
commissioner to direct the decision-making process, but her involvement in
the implementation, in this case communicating the results of her investi-
gation and directing the personnel changes, was her choice. Her participation communicated the finality of the decision, which would not have been
communicated as clearly or authoritatively by a subordinate. After announcing the decision,

> I did write a memorandum to all social services employees across the state,
> explaining what was done [and] why it was done. We met with regional
> directors and gave them a full accounting so that they could go back in their
> regions and county directors and everything and try to [remain] calm,
> because I mean the whole state was aroused over the way things were hap-
> pening, and we did salvage our credibility. We didn't fire anybody, we did dis-
> cipline, we think appropriately, all the people involved. . . . We did bring a
> counselor from Memphis up to work with that social services staff to try to
> again give them some immediate help in recognizing proper ways to handle
> cases, and I . . . believe that we have community support for our program.

A middle manager would not have sufficient positional authority to draw
in the stakeholders, to take the quick, arbitrary steps necessary to restore the
agency's credibility to its employees or to the community in which the incident took place. The commissioner's personal implementation can communicate legitimacy and finality in high-profile decisions.

Cheerleading for Legitimacy and Diffuse Emotional Support

Activities aimed at motivating employees to perform well are a standard tool
among the executives interviewed here. Department employees have seen
commissioners come and go, so an unhappy or a disgruntled employee can
do the minimum necessary, sit tight, hunker down, and wait for the commissioner to leave. Consequently, a key issue for a department executive is
structuring policies and fostering an organizational environment that
encourages the department's civil servants to implement plans and policies
willingly and effectively.

The goal is to create a work environment that inspires extra effort and pride in accomplishment. If an employee wakes each morning dreading the thought of going to the job, then that employee will not likely give extra effort to do a good job. A cynical "Good enough for government work" will hang like a cloud over the employee's head. Conversely, if an employee feels positive about the work situation, perceives respectful treatment by those in authority, then the employee is likely to work conscientiously. Creating an environment where the staff *wants* to carry out the executive's wishes makes the job of the chief executive easier. Actions to enhance commitment target emotions—creating and sustaining the belief that not only is this a good place to work but also that this commissioner deserves a decent effort.

Susan Simons, commissioner of the Department of General Services, who focused her efforts on changing the culture of her department from "control" to "service," describes her activities aimed at that goal:

> I think that now that I am comfortable with it, that I am not doing justice to how uncomfortable I did feel in the beginning. . . . You cannot help but feel a little silly talking about "Great Service" every time you get up, but I forced myself to do that.

Darrell Akins went outside his circle of immediate subordinates within the agency to communicate with frontline workers to link their performance to the overall success of the agency:

> I always told the senior staff that I really didn't care about their morale. They were making enough money; they had enough prestige and highfalutin titles to take care of their own morale.[5] I did worry about technicians and clerks. I spent a lot of personal time just going through the department, just sitting down and talking with individual employees and explaining to them why what they were doing was important. Why they were so necessary for the classification system to work, that they had to do their part.

Driving down the interstate, Commissioner Farris of the Department of Transportation spotted a DOT employee mowing along the side of the road. The commissioner pulled over and identified himself:

> I told him that it looks good. . . . "It's important to keep our roadsides mowed. You're doing a good job." And I've had them tell me, "I've worked here for twenty-seven years, and you're the first damn road commissioner I've ever seen."

The point was not performance appraisal—whether the employee was performing competently. At issue here was the executive's ability to encourage an employee by taking the time to stop and speak. It does not guarantee an enhanced effort, but it cannot hurt, and it probably helps. Such small, symbolic acts become news and travel throughout the organization to communicate to the employees that the commissioner shows them respect.

In addition to praise and support, motivating employees to improve performance may translate into a commissioner giving small prizes, instituting an award club, or formally recognizing good work by small rewards contingent on achieving a performance standard in line with the commissioner's goals. Commissioner Farris would award small "T" lapel pins for meritorious service. These rewards complement the picnics, retreats, or impromptu visits and speeches to raise morale by offering symbolic attention from the apex of the pyramid to frontline and middle-level workers.

Executives exhorted, cajoled, appealed, and generally acted as cheerleaders, encouraging their employees to subscribe to the department's mission. In the process of getting employees to feel good about their jobs, many of the commissioners toured work sites, both at the home office and in the field. These activities performed by the commissioners were aimed at the implementation process. They believed that they could enhance the agency's goals and make their job easier if they created a work climate that encouraged employees to feel good about working for the department.

Consciously Avoiding Implementation Activity

As previously mentioned, the average tenure of cabinet members is very short—only two and a half years nationally. Any changes that an executive proposes need to be entrenched in the bureaucracy to enhance the likelihood that the changes will endure a leadership transition. Commissioner Farris wanted to change the decision processes within the Department of Transportation by encouraging cross-departmental decision groups. He considered these quality circles one of his major contributions to the operations of the department. When asked how he went about installing these, he said, "I assigned the task to an assistant commissioner." But why remain aloof from your major initiative? He indicated that the assistant commissioner had been there long before Farris had shown up, and that he would be there long after Farris left. If the assistant commissioner considered the program his, then it would likely outlive the present administration. Farris chose implementation strategies carefully and targeted policy longevity with his implementation strategy.

Executive Implementation: Summary

Within the agency the commissioner is at the top, not nested in the middle of a dense environment. Implementation on some issues can be accomplished by directly and unequivocally telling the subordinates to "do it." The commissioner can command, and commanding especially works when implementation is direct and simple: spend/do not spend, hire/fire, do this job/do that job. The commissioner's position also allows him or her to speak authoritatively outside the agency and to provide emotional support and comfort to employees at lower levels of the departmental pyramid.

Executives have more access than middles both inside and outside the organization. The higher up the chain of command, the less dense the network of clearances needed to obtain a decision, and the easier the access to the people necessary to complete the task. Ease of implementation was a consideration for executives. Tasks normally implemented at middle levels of the organization often can be accomplished more efficiently and more easily by the commissioner. The spraying story from the Department of Agriculture showed the obstacles faced by a middle manager who had to assemble funds from various accounts to pay for a project when the money was not available for another three months. That departmental commissioner ignored the heavy burden placed on the middle manager. Agency employees were inconvenienced because the executive did not think through the decision's implementation implications. The effective executives that we interviewed were skilled at thinking through their decisions, not only deciding what to do but also asking themselves how implementation could be accomplished most efficiently.

Visibility and reputation aid implementation. Commissioners have more prominence than most middle managers, and they can enhance their personal reputations and the effectiveness of middle managers struggling to implement inside the agency by regularly emphasizing the agency's current mission and objectives and supporting this talk by offering symbolic rewards for achievements and by showing appreciation for the work of frontline employees and supervisors.

CONCLUSIONS

Implementation is taking a policy or program and making it happen. Talking is the implementation activity common to both executives and middle managers; effective verbal communication is a vital management skill basic to all levels of management. Middle managers typically are embedded in a dense environment of stakeholders who need consulting, informing, cajoling, and convincing. Meetings and conversations are the daily activities that typify how middle managers implement. Paying attention to subordinates boosts morale and establishes a link between the manager and the subordinate so that employees will want to work for the manager. Personal contacts matter. A middle manager needs a strong network as insurance to deal with unexpected challenges, as shown by the insect-spraying story. The network builder pays attention to detail, listens carefully, and shows respect to coworkers.

Executives have two talking-style options not readily available to middle managers. First, executives can be directive when dealing with subordinates. Being directive can avoid costly delays and curb wrangling among stakeholders. Second, executives can build a supportive cadre of workers by speaking in supportive platitudes, bonding frontline employees to the mission and goals of the agency. Because they speak to some people they see only occasionally, commissioners can sometimes get by with vague generalities. Their purpose is not to carry on a substantive dialogue but to show respect for the employee as a valued member of the agency team. Middle managers can use this supportive communication style, but the message carries more weight when delivered by the commissioner.

The literature does not describe the executive as implementer. We find that the effective executive is a skillful, selective implementer. Outstanding commissioners must guard their time and implement selectively. Focusing implementation efforts on those policies and directives that have a short time frame and are heavily symbol-laden pays quick and significant dividends. Both executives and middle managers are involved in implementation, but implementing a policy or program operates very differently at the top of the hierarchy than it does at the middle.

Once the program is implemented, evaluation is the next, final step in the decision-making process.

SIX

Evaluation

EVALUATION IS NORMALLY USED to assess the outcome of an activity or the performance of someone doing an activity. Here the selection process defined managerial competence, and the stories were specified in advance as successful. Therefore, we are not evaluating managerial performance or assessing the outcome of a decision. We seek to understand the underlying strategies and behaviors used by the successful manager. What skills are used to accomplish these successful activities, and how do the skills of successful managers vary between the middle manager level and the executive level?

In surveying researchers of organizational effectiveness, Quinn and Rohrbaugh (1983, 365) posed the following question: "How do individual theorists and researchers actually think about the construct of effectiveness?" After multidimensional scaling of the responses, Quinn and Rohrbaugh arrived at a competing values model of organizational effectiveness organized along three dimensions: focus, structure, and means-ends. The "focus" dimension of the model locates the problem/opportunity as inside the organization or outside the organization. "Structure" divides the manager's behavioral emphasis into controlling the situation or taking a flexible, adaptive approach to obtain a desired outcome (see Figure 6.1).[1] Managers included in their stories the strategies and tactics they employed in achieving their success. In doing so, they revealed their management skills. We used this model to chart the strategies and behaviors of managers and executives.

Although an individual manager may emphasize a single pole on each dimension, the effective organization does not focus solely on one dimension but balances criteria both among the dimensions and between each pole of each dimension in the organization as a whole (Lawrence and Lorsch 1967). Managers may use multiple skills to accomplish their tasks and multiple criteria to

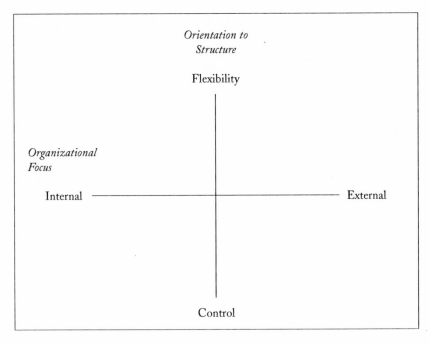

FIGURE 6.1
A Competing Values Approach to Organizational Effectiveness

Source: Quinn and Rohrbaugh (1983).

evaluate their work. The greater variety of problem-solving strategies, tactics, and outcome justifications that a manager or executive employs, the more textured the evaluation scheme and the broader the repertoire possessed by the manager.[2] In addition to analyzing decisions by the managers in terms of this classification scheme, we assess whether our executives and middle managers handle evaluation similarly or differently.

MIDDLE MANAGERS

Stories are divided into one of two focus categories: internally focused and externally focused. In situations involving an external focus, flexibility is the strategy of choice. Middle managers cannot use "control" to address the situation unless they have access to an external source of support. Only one of the externally focused stories told by the middle managers demonstrated control, and that was because the manager had the law backing his actions. Planning and goal setting, *means* typical of the rational model, were ignored. Middle managers, buffeted by pressures on all sides, appear to think that for achieving their goals communicating and building organization morale are more effective. Internally focused situations lie within the sphere of the middle manager's authority, so the manager has the option of using control, flexibility, or some combination of the two.

External Focus: Flexibility

To find placements for his long-term care patients whose residential care was no longer eligible for state reimbursement, a mental health institute superintendent had to locate host families or nursing homes to care for these elderly mentally ill whose only means of payment was their federal monthly check. He had to uncover and work with local providers in order to meet the federal standards necessary for reimbursement. After much work, he was successful in recruiting and helping people figure out how to modify their homes to meet the federal standards. Middle managers rarely control the situations for which they are responsible. They have to be flexible in order to achieve their objectives.

A Department of Conservation middle manager describes the problem he faced:

> [A few years back] we lost our entire federal funding to our reclamation program, and we went from a $3 million a year budget to zero; it was quite frustrating. Well, it's a hard way to start a successful story, starting at ground zero. My part of it . . . was trying to decide what we were going to do. We immediately contacted the federal agency that inherited the regulatory program, [and] offered [them] the experienced service of eleven staff members through intergovernmental personnel act agreements, and they accepted. Of course, they were in dire need of some experienced reclamation and regulatory folks, which I was fortunate enough to have on board, and as a result we all went on and reported to the federal funding agency. Nobody missed a paycheck.

The manager's primary goals—keeping the program running and his people paid, measurable objectives—were successfully met by being flexible in the face of potential disaster for his organization. He could not control the decision of the federal government, but having experienced employees present in the field when the federal government needed immediate assistance afforded him an opportunity to negotiate from a strong position.

The Tennessee Department of Labor had responsibility for the Federal Job Training Partnership Act. A director-level middle manager said this:

> The assistant commissioner wanted me to take a look at what it would take to get a marketing program going, and so I worked on that.

After recounting a series of battles with other state agencies, the middle manager concludes the story:

> We even had to have the commissioner before the publications committee to talk to them about the whole issue of revenue and what is revenue, stadiums versus bringing in new revenues. We won our last battle on it; it's in place and we have the three public service announcements showing.

The Department of Labor manager had no power over the other state agencies. They were outside his control. Persuasion was the only tool. The middle manager, backed by his commissioner, was successful in convincing the external stakeholders who were holding up progress on the program.

A director in DHS was having her audit findings on agencies that contract with the state overturned on appeal, which is not a desirable or comfortable outcome. The audit monitors from fiscal services were beyond her control. She had to correct the situation and convince the audit monitors that the situation was corrected.

> When I first started to work in the contract office in the Department of Human Services, . . . we were having a lot of trouble making our audit findings stick. That is, when fiscal services reviewed them, they would forgive the agencies, and it was hurting the morale of the auditors . . . so we decided the three divisions (fiscal services and community services and audit) needed to get to know each other better . . . learn what each other was doing; so we scheduled a staff retreat last year and all of us did the craziest skits you've ever seen. But the message got across.
>
> Very seldom now do we have audit findings that don't stick; in fact, a lot of times when auditors are in the field, they'll call fiscal services and say, "Now, how will you interpret this if we write this?" And it's made a stronger relationship in the department with the contract agencies and with the monitors. That has worked out so well that many times now we take monitors along on the audits, really been good for all of us.

Getting to know people from another agency, seeing the situation from their perspective as a result of interaction, and communicating their perspective by silly skits both broke the emotional ice and developed mutually shared understandings, which resulted in productivity and efficiency.

In each of these stories, the success was obvious: the mental health patients were placed in homes located nearby, the Department of Conservation employees were transferred to the federal payroll, the Department of Labor ads were running, and the auditors' attitudes toward supervisors were now positive. Success was obvious, and the results were measurable.

External Focus: Control

Occasionally a middle manager is in a control position vis-à-vis an external environment. When the communications company Viacom came to Nashville it agreed to provide free connections to a number of public institutions, including the training academy for the Department of Safety. However, Viacom never delivered on its commitment until confronted by a middle manager who taught at the police academy.

> I managed to get hold of a copy of the metro ordinance and they [Viacom] started telling me they weren't going to be doing this because of the expense. I started quoting the statute to them. It was a long drawn-out procedure, but to make a long story short Viacom installed the cable at no cost to us. They were wondering how I knew so much about the law, I guess. . . . I was up against not a governmental bureaucracy but against a bureaucracy that was much larger than myself and [yet I] managed to get it done.

This middle manager's legal expertise brought a measurable win—wiring the academy—a rare example of policy success by a middle manager dealing with a powerful actor in the external environment by using a control style.

Internal Focus: Control

For internal situations, the middle manager has a choice—either flexibility or control. One mental health middle manager walked into a situation where three supervisors could not get along. One resigned, another transferred, the third remained.

> The individual remaining, a lady who had been in state government a long time, great technician, had a staff of fifteen, but that woman had no interpersonal skills, absolutely none. Her main tactic was management by fear and intimidation, and *I* was intimidated. She and I had numerous conversations about the way she treated her subordinates; and after repeated warnings, I had to encourage her to move on, and did that without any job replacement or anything else. But you know, I guess the thing that I learned then more than any time in my whole career was that when you take decent subordinates and they share in that particular problem, then they also share in the benefits, is that it's incredible how quickly they'll pitch in to get the job done.

That was a painful decision, because the manager's preferred style is flexibility and decisions made by consensus. Workplace morale and performance were so bad that he went against his preferred style and forfeited a position rather than continue with the intimidating supervisor. The arbitrary decision (exercising control) by firing the supervisor was defined as a success, because after the supervisor left, the frontline employees performed effectively without a supervisor. The office was more comfortable for the staff after the intimidating employee's departure, which could have been demonstrated by workplace satisfaction indicators, and the manager reported enhanced performance as well.

The internally focused stories were not always easily categorized as examples of either flexibility or control, since some managers used both control and flexibility in order to be successful. A prison warden articulates his measurable results:

> In the five and a half years I was warden at this 400-bed minimum security prison, we never had one work stoppage, never had one inmate that got killed, we only had one stabbing in five and a half years. I can't remember one case where one of my officers was physically assaulted. Now, that doesn't mean we didn't have problems, escapes and certain things like that. I guess what I'm saying, to me I think that's somewhat of a success story. When I measure my style, I look at things like that.

This manager focused internally. When speaking of evaluation, the control aspect dominated his concern, because his responsibility was to keep inmates confined and safe, and prison personnel safe. He used statistics to support his statement of increased effectiveness. Safety measures indicate the use of control; the fact that there was no work stoppage suggests flexibility. Elsewhere in the interview this warden indicates responsibility devolved to others in his organization. As the manager of a prison system, we presume that control takes prominence as the means for achieving stability and effectiveness. However, at a prison, as in any effective organization, some flexibility will likely be needed.

The Viacom, intimidating supervisor, and correction stories described situations where control was important in achieving organizational success. Each middle manager backed his claim to effectiveness with hard evidence.

Internal Focus: Flexibility

Often an internal problem was the low morale or negative atmosphere of the work unit. A social services middle manager sought to create an environment in which employees felt comfortable. Evidence to indicate success included such statements as "people have stopped complaining," "better acceptance of decisions," "the more inclusive, participatory style has spread," and "the workers used to say 'welcome to the pits,' they don't say that anymore."

A director in the Department of Agriculture faced internal dissension and poor performance.

> I'm director of the food and dairy division, and that division was a combination of the food and drug section and our dairy analysis section. They merged two divisions and made one. The previous director was from the food and drug division, so the dairy division felt like they were stepchildren, and the program was really going down. The assistant director for the dairy division and the commissioner didn't get along at all; so a lot of things that were asked for weren't received, and the dairy program was falling down. So that was a priority right at first: give confidence and support to the dairy inspectors. We've seen a lot of turnaround . . . about six months ago, we were running number one in the Southeast for regulatory scores.

The objective evidence of regional regulatory ratings supports the contention of outstanding performance. From the story it appears that the manager's attention and energy were concentrated internally to build up the morale of the unit. Success was measured in terms of an external focus.

A corrections middle manager coming into a new position in central office turned his energies toward creating a more inclusive, less contentious unit. He had a participatory, relaxed style that devolved substantial budget responsibility to subordinates. The manager saw himself as a resource, not as a ruling authority. This choice of a flexible style was vindicated some time later when relationships between the field and central office in the Department of Correction became so contentious that the commissioner offered field people the option of their existing chain of command or skipping over the director level to communicate directly with the assistant commissioner.

> I think it's a success . . . [because of] my style, being a resource. The commissioner gave the wardens a chance to make a decision: do they want to change who they report to; do they feel like they're being suffocated? Well, the adult [facility] wardens picked that they would rather go to the assistant commissioner; mine didn't want to do that.

This middle manager's flexible style was comfortable to his subordinates, who responded positively by choosing to report to him rather than to go to a higher authority, the assistant commissioner. Effectiveness was not measured by productivity indicators but by the job satisfaction and high morale demonstrated by a reluctance to select reporting directly to a higher authority when offered the option. The food and dairy manager documented success with statistical evidence; the correction manager could point to the fact that his subordinates chose to report to him rather than directly to the next higher level, which would have given them greater reach within the agency.

The effective middle managers we interviewed, although sometimes using control as a means to achieve their objectives, preferred flexibility, or facilitation. Taking control is the less-preferred option, to be used when necessary, as in a prison, or a last resort. The mental health manager who fired a subordinate was forced by circumstances to go against his preferred style of flexibility and consensus. After losing two out of three supervisors, and a deteriorating work performance from the third unit, he needed to take control, so he did. Firing the incompetent employee occurred only after "numerous conversations . . . repeated warnings." The word "firing" was not used. The manager said, "I had to encourage her to move on." It appears that these highly successful middle managers saw flexibility and facilitation creating cohesiveness and high morale within the workplace and resulting in high performance.

The most highly developed middle manager skills were negotiating and facilitating, honed by a constant diet of meetings with stakeholders and colleagues with whom persuasion was the route to achieving goals. It is natural that they would fall back on these well-developed skills to raise underperforming subordinates to an acceptable standard. Being controlling, using less-familiar skills when the preferred skills do not accomplish the objective, takes some of these competent facilitators out of their comfort zone.

Middle managers focusing internally found hard measures to substantiate their success. "We set the deadline, and we met it." Some set measurable goals and challenged their subordinates to meet them, and as a result "it [the new program] reduced the errors by 68 percent." Using hard data to justify the outcome as a success does not mean that the manager employed an inflexible, control approach to structure. Internally focused managers generally preferred flexible rather than control methods. Nor would using control tactics mean the absence of flexibility in their managerial style. Overall, middle managers prefer flexibility to control, whether focused internally or externally.

Multiple Dimensions

Some middle managers told stories that fit into more than one of the skill categories. A new manager was hired for an educational facility in DHS. He emphasized both training and assessment of his staff, firing those who would not get with the new agenda of personal responsibility and appropriate respect for clients. Reflecting on the situation over the past five years, he related:

> The success rate turned around drastically and quickly. This year, and this is after five years [of] operation, really hit the peak. In the center that [originally] served probably 100 to 190 people; with the same amount of staff we serve over a thousand. We ran an 80 percent success rate, people completing programs, and that's a 45 percent increase over the last two years.

He used hard evidence to support a record of achievement. Although the manager's emphasis on staff training to achieve growth, efficiency, and productivity included both hard and soft methods, the manager appears to be in control, for there is no indication of devolving responsibility outside of his office.

A middle manager in DHS claimed that he "got funding for program" (flexible/external), and he also obtained "secure backing and ownership by the board" (external/control). Further, the atmosphere is better (internal/flexibility), and productivity is up (external/flexibility); errors were reduced (internal/control) and gave the county three more working days by eliminating some paperwork (external control). This middle manager proposed a totally new system for entering and tracking welfare recipients. This problem-solving behavior reflects the kind of broad visioning and coalition building with stakeholders more typical of executives than middle managers. His story that follows is also unique because it incorporates initiative and risk taking that involved people above his level and outside of his agency.

> Anytime bank tellers were catching on and real popular. They'd been around for a while, but all of a sudden everybody started using them, and I came up with the idea of putting any anytime teller in each of the county offices. . . . It would allow the counties to put their data in the system at that level and get out of batching and mailing and a lot of turnover time, so I came in and presented it to the staff, to a very small group of what I call my brains. It's the right arms that work real close. We got excited about it and started working together as a team and just brainstormed. We had some equipment that we were using in six of the regional centers that we have across the state and we said, "All right, let's just put it in a lab and develop the software that we can do totally in DHS." I started talking and selling this concept to other people. At that time Darrell Akins was our deputy commissioner in DHS and Darrell was the first one that listened to it. I was able to bend his ear. It was technical and he wasn't heavy into data processing, but he looked at me and said, "You believe in this?" And I said, "Yes, I do." He said, "You keep working on it and you just keep selling it and keep getting people to talk to you, cause if you believe in it, it's a good idea, just keep working on it."
>
> So I did. This whole concept had to do with a different philosophy than was in F&A, [which was] to centralize the computer system. . . . They had never dealt with that and didn't want to deal with it. I have letters in the file that say, "This is the world's largest band-aid. Your department is hemorrhaging and you're talking about network, that's a very expensive kind of thing." One afternoon I entertained six of their people [from F&A] coming over to talk about this project. The whole thing was a stall tactic, slowing down, get him off track, run him through a bunch of hoops . . . I got real support from my immediate supervisor, who was the assistant commissioner in administrative services, Lewis Harris. Lewis is not highly skilled at technical

data processing, he'd be one of the first people to tell you that. [It] came down to he and I talking one day face-to-face. He said, "This is risky, you're wanting to go against the establishment." I said, "Yes, it is risky." "Will it work?" When he asked that big question and looked at me right in the eye there's only two of you in the room. The answer meant a lot. I said, "Yeah, it will work." So he came on board then. That was risky for both of us. He made it perfectly clear that the answer was going out on a limb, and there wasn't going to be but one person out on that limb, and I accepted that going in. So he bought into the project then, and he did one tremendous thing, and I couldn't have pulled this off, but he called the assistant commissioner then, by the name of Ron Dickey, he is over [at] F&A, he said, "I want you to go with me one afternoon," and he didn't set it up much more than that, just "I want you to spend the afternoon with me." I had gone through enough loops to have a county set up as a pilot, and he took Ron Dickey one afternoon and went to Spring Hill, Tennessee, Robinson County, and showed it to Ron. Ron got excited, he said, "You've got something." So Ron came back, and in very short order he got his people turned around. It took that kind of emphasis, it took the two assistant commissioners, and all of a sudden I got a few more people want to listen to me and agree with it so we went out on a competitive bid.

Ron was very oriented toward one vendor, and I didn't care for that, [but] that did not bother me, the project I knew would be a benefit to the agency, and I didn't care what hardware, that wasn't important at this time, it was getting the concept in. So we went through the purchasing and procurement. To make a long story short, we got to network in all ninety-five counties. It's been labeled the best thing since sliced bread. It gave the county three more working days, no U.S. mail, it reduced the errors that they're making in the counties by 68 percent. In other words, we got a machine in the counties that edits the data as you put it in, where before it was a total manual effort that had gone through the mail, so we were catching 68 percent of the errors before the data ever left the county, and they have a direct link. The network is what is important because you have a communication line going to the county that has evolved where we first put a terminal out there, then we put the printer out there, then there was additional need for additional work stations in some of the counties and now in fifty-four counties we have microcomputers that are all hooked to this network.

You can evaluate it several ways. We kept all of our suspense file statistics of how many errors they had before quest and when we did a comparison afterwards—that would give us numbers and statistics. That's how come I know 68 percent is a good number of errors. So you do that kind of thing. Most of the evaluation comes on what those people said and what they're saying to other people. Commissioner Puett got a field report from every region when she was the commissioner, and they'd talk about it and those things, positive things. When regional people would come out of Atlanta and do a performance evaluation on the county, it would come up. All of a sudden we were getting invited to southeastern regional states to talk about the project, this sort of thing, so you get that kind of evaluation that it's a good project. And ISSD [the F&A responsible unit] is very proud of it now.

The director of information services in DHS came up with the idea of computers in field offices so that client data entered in the field would go directly into a central system at agency headquarters. No conflict surfaced with peers within DHS, so there was not a dense environment inside the agency. However, this idea challenged the state agency responsible for control of state government computing. Density occurred in the environment outside of the agency. The density he encountered in the wider environment would have been present even had this director been a commissioner. One agency (DHS) was encroaching on the turf of another, F&A, the most prestigious department in state government. The DHS director was able to overcome obstacles by strategically planning and implementing a strategy—building support incrementally by working through people within his network—first, his assistant commissioner in DHS, who was convinced by the presentation, and who set up an appointment and went with him to an assistant commissioner in the computer agency. Armed with strong support from these two allies, he went back to his own commissioner, who was easily convinced and therefore allowed the program to be implemented.

A middle manager seeking to innovate can come up with a creative idea and convince an executive of the idea's worth. The story of this director and the automated teller machines illustrates the number of gates that must be negotiated in order to achieve success. This innovative activity by a middle manager demands commitment and extra work from one's subordinates and exceptional networking and credibility outside of the agency. In terms of evaluation, the director was focused solely on efficiency and effectiveness and employed the means of all four quadrants to reach his goal.

Summary: Middle Manager Evaluation

Although middle managers could articulate their accomplishments in a measurable way, which fits their training and reward structure, not all cases involved counting things, and often the success was so obvious to the manager that no hard data were provided. Nor did all evaluation fall into the rational-analytic category. Emotions played a big role; the feeling of accomplishment counted for the middle managers as they told their stories. Their personal evaluation of the effectiveness of their activities was rated on a scale that was less statistics-based and more emotion-based. They were successful in their efforts because they felt good about the outcome, and the problem went away; the internal environment no longer was filled with complaining and dissension.

When dealing internally, it appears that middle managers would shift along the flexibility-control dimension as they thought necessary. Middle managers have to deal effectively both externally and internally. Their dominant management style is flexibility/devolvement, discussing matters and coming to a consensus decision, whether among peers or subordinates. They *must* use flexibility with peers and those of higher rank; they use it with subordinates by choice. They can and do employ control tactics, but generally control is not their preferred style.

Because middles are located in a hierarchical organization and are accountable to superiors for their performance, statements such as the following are used: thirty-four thousand employees reclassified without a hitch, cable installed at no cost, 45 percent increase in the success rate over the past two years, never had a work stoppage or an inmate killed, number one department in the Southeast for regulatory scores, seldom have audit findings that do not stick, three ads running, three days more time. Middles use this hard evidence to demonstrate their management skill to peers and superiors. They perform competently; they know it, and often can use numbers to prove it, if necessary.

The public image of a state-level middle manager is perhaps an employee who narrow-mindedly emphasizes rules, who rigidly does what one's boss dictates, and who expects conformity to rules by subordinates and the public. This image of the control-oriented bureaucrat is diametrically opposite from the behaviors exhibited by the competent middle managers we interviewed. As middle managers, their primary challenges come from dealing with people whom they cannot control. They must develop facilitator and negotiator skills in order to be successful. Having been recognized and rewarded for having developed these competencies, they adopt flexibility and negotiation as their primary strategies when facing any problem. When flexibility will not work, they must resort to control, a managerial skill less comfortable to them, but one that must be brought out, dusted off, and used from time to time.

Middle manager leadership often fits the characterizations of Weick (1978) in "The Spines of Leaders," Granovetter (1973) in "The Strength of Weak Ties," and Collins (2001) in "Level 5 Leadership." Attending more than visibly acting, listening more than talking, and paradox more than a singular focus describe these leadership qualities. Middle managers can be effective leaders by developing these skills, and some demonstrate their abilities by ranging over multiple dimensions in the Quinn and Rohrbaugh (1983) typology.

EXECUTIVES

Middle managers were likely to use "we" to characterize their management activities, while executives preferred "I." This concurs with our findings in chapter 4. Middle managers are ensconced in a dense structure, so by necessity they spend a lot of time in meetings. It is natural that the successful program outcome would be conceived as a group effort by the middle managers, hence the "we." Executives, at the top of the agency hierarchy, are less beholden to others when deciding what to do, hence "I" rather than "we" is more usual.

Executives' stories also illustrate the range of competing values operating at the executive level, as we will demonstrate later, but the categories are even less clear-cut than those articulated by the middle managers. When evaluating a program or policy, each commissioner used evaluation criteria that covered multiple quadrants of the Quinn and Rohrbaugh (1983) model. They would evaluate their success using statistics, assessment by outsiders, cost estimates, employee morale, or their personal judgment of performance. Often they thought the evaluation question moot. Obviously the outcome was successful; raising the question was to them unnecessary, perhaps even a challenge to their assessment that the story illustrated managerial success.

Internal Focus: Control

Commissioner Farris during our interview told of cutting inventory, monitoring the use of equipment such as water jugs, spare parts, and gloves, and personally signing off on every purchase order. He evaluated his overall performance at the Department of Transportation as follows:

> The first year we took over a million dollars off the inventory. That million dollars went right out into road projects instead of sitting on the shelves gathering dust. . . . Did we give good value for the dollars that we had? Were our programs well-planned and well thought out, were they reasonably well executed, did we come away with good value received for what we've expended? And I've spent a lot of money. In the four years I've been here, there's been some $20-odd million flowing through my department—did we really give a good value for that? I hope to heck we did.

Farris focused on the outcome attributable to the internal functioning of the organization: Did we give good value? Were programs well planned, well thought out, reasonably executed? Farris demonstrates a control orientation to structure as he described an inventory reduction program that he originated.

External Focus: Flexibility

A flexibility/external focus was used to evaluate a physical plant management initiative that involved a public-private partnership in building construction.

> It was cost-effective. The agencies are now housed together instead of all over town. There is room to grow.

External Focus: Control

In the Better Schools program, Commissioner McElrath used numbers to illustrate his success.

> We've just completed giving a test for children in grades 3, 6, and 8 in basic skills, and given the Stanford Achievement in grades 5–7. Now we at least have a baseline for those youngsters, and hopefully local boards of education will pass this, saying how does my school compare with the national level, where's the standard of the state? . . . When 120,000 youngsters have already received fifteen lessons in computer skills, and when a great majority of those youngsters say this is exciting, that's evaluation . . . 39,000 teachers are making at least \$1,000 a year more than the previous year as a result of having climbed the first level. More than 1,200 will make from \$2–7,000 more on the next level.

The effectiveness categories used by Quinn and Rohrbaugh (1983) fit, but it is a stretch. It is particularly hard to categorize the effectiveness criteria because of the facility of the executives as they moved among evaluation schemes—the program is effective if you look at it this way, it also works if you measure it another way, and so on. Clearly, the executives did not limit themselves to a single-evaluation criterion. They employed multiple criteria and did so with ease. The evaluation strategies of executives did not easily fit on the Quinn and Rohrbaugh (1983) dimensions. We set up the following additional evaluative categories: Avoiding Controversy and Negative Publicity, Policy Longevity and Stability, and the Wallenda Factor.

Avoiding Controversy and Negative Publicity

We have separated out this category because it demonstrates a concern that we often heard from the executives and did not hear from the middle managers. The commissioners did not want to see the name of their agency in the newspaper or on the television newscast. Commissioner of Correction Steve Norris indicated that under no circumstances was an article in the newspaper about the Correction Department a good thing. Only when there was a problem did the press feature the department. The commissioner characterized his job as making sure that the Correction Department did not make the papers. While a commissioner would like to control what the media says, this is impossible. Nor will being flexible prevent an unexpected negative result. A desire for effectiveness was juxtaposed with fear of a possible political explosion. Danger lay just below the surface as the executives took risks to achieve effectiveness in state government. Commissioner Akins, Department of Personnel, described his feelings:

There were a lot of political risks. I was always scared to death that we would become a campaign issue. . . . Well, you're sort of like walking through a minefield, because you were, always. I never worried about it a whole lot, I mean, you just accept it in the political world.

Commissioner Puett's difficult child abuse situation consumed the commissioner full time for more than a month. Stakeholders were arrayed on all sides—some arguing that the employees be fired, others demanding that the employees be exonerated. Feelings ran high, and there was little middle ground. Success was defined by the commissioner as follows:

I guess I considered it successful in that all of those parties to it, and all of them had conflicting interests of different kinds, all accepted it and went on from there, there has been no negative fallout after it was over. It isn't that they liked it or were happy about it, some thought the penalty was too severe, some thought that, whatever, but the fact was that we did it, those workers, that counselor is still with us, that county director is still with us, they are productive, capable employees, I don't think you could determine it was successful right after it was over, I think only time showed whether that was the right thing to do, and I think there has been sufficient time now to conclude that it was right.

Her decision ended the controversy. All sides accepted the result. An important concern of the commissioner—that the agency could continue to work effectively in that county—was maintained. Having an emotional issue evaporate without rancor on any side is a positive, difficult to achieve outcome, and the fact that the issue did not blow up and become a statewide media event was a positive indicator of the commissioner's success.

Policy Longevity and Stability

Policy longevity and stability are important, wished-for outcomes that were implicitly desired but rarely verbalized by commissioners, and never by middle managers. With the public-sector executive likely to remain in office less than three years, an important concern is how one can both be effective in managing the ongoing challenges and also lay a foundation for better management in the years to come. In the words of Commissioner Farris:

There is an ingredient in the system that is filled with inertia, and you've got to recognize it's there. They [subordinates] will just wait you out, cause they know you won't be there forever. That's part of the challenge. I think we've got to, through communicative skills or whatever, try to push things in as best you can. . . . If you overdo that, the system will rebel against you, and you lose ground that you've gained. I've seen that happen in good, skillful private-sector managers that are used to pushing the buck and getting a response. Trying to manage the same way [in the public sector]—you can't do that because of the way the system exists. The vast majority of those people [subordinates] will be there long after I'm gone; won't ever see me again. Some other character will show up. . . . I instituted quality circles in the DOT. . . . I brought it up to my managers—that we have got to watch and see that everybody doesn't say, "This is another commissioner's scheme, and he'll be gone." I had to make sure that if we instigated this [quality circles], it was structured in such a way that it had some stability and longevity.

Able commissioners look not only internally and externally, to flexibility and control, to means and ends, but to temporary versus enduring solutions. When faced with a problem of excessive inventory, Farris signed every purchase order as a stopgap measure to get employees to focus momentarily on inventory. Long term, a computerized inventory system would provide efficient control. Farris wanted intradepartmental, enduring, cross-functional teams as a means for engendering ongoing effectiveness inside of the agency. This participatory management scheme was assigned to an assistant commissioner to administer, housed lower in the organization to increase the likelihood that it would gain traction within the agency and survive the commissioner's tenure.

Personnel Commissioner Martha Olsen demonstrated a similar sensitivity to the temporal dimension by involving her career managers in reorganizing the department.

I'm only a person who has an opportunity to rent the house that they live in; it was very important to me that when they got a new tenant they had a good organization to be able to carry on, and I wanted them to participate. There were no secrets, and I didn't have any grand schemes or any grand design.

Middle managers did not bring up temporality as an issue to be considered. Middle managers have too little control over their environment for stability and longevity policy issues to be relevant to them.

Commissioner Norris arrived a bit late for our interview. In chatting prior to commencing the interview, the commissioner said that he had been investigating an incident at the main prison.[3] After talking on-site to all of the parties involved, yes, he had decided how he would handle the matter, but he had not yet announced his decision. First he wanted to think about his larger agenda. How could he incorporate into his decision on the small, immediate incident a component that would further larger, long-term change at the main prison? He would wait to give his response to the immediate incident until he had decided how his response to that incidental matter could be woven into an action that could further his larger agenda. The competent commissioner looks for every incident requiring attention, however minor, as an opportunity to leverage a major agenda item.

The likelihood that the policy or program would become part of the fabric of the department was an evaluative criterion used by some executives. That stability and longevity would be associated with their initiatives was an additional consideration some executives took seriously. The strategies designed to outlive the executive might look downright inefficient if the time dimension were not considered. To have the commissioner signing every purchase order sounds like micromanaging; the same executive touts his participatory management/problem-solving teams as the key priority of his administration, and yet he removes himself from the project soon after it was initiated. But if the goal of the strategy is stability and longevity, then the strategies are brilliant. Linking vision to evaluation criteria is an important executive competency.

The Wallenda Factor

The "Wallenda factor" was a term coined by Bennis and Nanus (1985) to describe the "can-do" attitude of successful managers, "the capacity to embrace positive goals, to pour one's energies into the task, not into looking behind and dredging up excuses for past events" (Bennis and Nanus 1985, 71). Karl Wallenda, the famous tightrope walker, performed daring feats around the world and fell to his death only when he started thinking about failing rather than about succeeding. Although public-sector executives live in an environment filled with risk, they do not let their minds dwell upon the possibility of failure. All commissioners stated a highly positive overall evaluation of their tenure as department executives. Few admitted experiencing failure in anything that they attempted to accomplish.[4]

> I was trying to think of a policy issue that I have (lost). I don't think that I have lost one yet.

> I made a list of twelve things that I wanted to accomplish—most of them are completed or on their way.

> We had a long-term tax plan to put a penny on the sales tax; we ended up doing it half a cent for two years . . . it worked, it just needed a year for the legislators to justify themselves.

These positive evaluations were both a concrete assessment of their job accomplishments and an attitude toward their leadership skills. They believed in their own competence; they did not doubt their abilities. To avoid failure in legislative initiatives, the executives have backup strategies. They can offer a slightly different version of their proposal to the legislature the following year, or they can use administrative regulations to implement a policy initiative without legislation. The following comments demonstrate turning losses into victories.

> I was already chalking it up in the loss column until we began working through the points in the bill and looking at regulations. . . . By Christmas, we'll have 90 percent of what we would have had by law and will wind up with consolidation of the department and the constituency groups with a major change in how the department looks at quality care in nursing homes. . . . So we will have done far more to protect the patients than we would ever have done just by [a] simple act of legislation. A bad legislative result, but a good outcome in terms of ultimate public policy . . . I feel we did win.

> The Tennessee Teachers Association objected to . . . ; the delay resulted in a more comprehensive program.

> The result [of the controversy] is better thought out and longer lasting. We will be short a couple of things that we would have had with legislation. But there is always another year.

Sometimes the commissioner's statements strained credulity—a commissioner contending that no one was unhappy after the department was restructured, or another blithely saying that there had been a complete attitude change during the executive's tenure. While unlikely accomplished in full, the statements indicate that these executives have a "Wallenda attitude."

Positive self-regard was characteristic of all the executives, and a high evaluation of one's skills and competencies translates into leadership self-confidence that can turn a follower's indifference to enthusiasm. A self-confident leader who proclaims to subordinates "I win them all" can be more inspiring than an executive who offers perhaps a more realistic assessment: "I win some, and I lose some." Middle managers want to work for an executive who is a winner, and these executives all believed that they were winners.

Hayward and Hambrick (1997) have identified hubris, or exaggerated pride or self-confidence, as an explanatory factor in risky acquisition decisions by private-sector executives. Confident executives make bold decisions. The executives working for Alexander considered themselves bold and confident managers, and demonstrated this most notably in their discussions of evaluation. This is not to say that the executives studied here are infected with a lack of humility, but rather that the self-confidence displayed by the executives is an important, positive characteristic in executive behavior. These executives displayed high levels of self-confidence.

The evaluation process gets tangled up with the executive's self-confidence—it is the self-confidence that inspires others to follow. Leadership behaviors are paradoxical: the manager needs a realistic assessment of the organization's capabilities in order to achieve success in meeting challenges, but at the same time the manager needs to demonstrate a confident attitude to motivate subordinates to follow enthusiastically. All of the executives in our study demonstrated the self-confidence to generate enthusiasm among employees located down the administrative hierarchy.

COMPARING EXECUTIVES AND MIDDLE MANAGERS ON EVALUATION

Middle managers used fewer evaluative indicators than did executives. Middle managers deftly cited statistics to demonstrate that they were successful. Executives might cite statistics when pressed to do so, but they would attribute their success to a variety of reasons reflecting multiple dimensions. Executives told longer, more complex stories and approached problems from multiple perspectives. It appears that the number of categories considered in the manager's decision is influenced by position, the experience of the individual, and administrative ability.

Collectively, middle managers describe success criteria over the full range of the typology; however, individual middle managers use fewer effectiveness categories and dimensions to describe their successful activity than do executives. Executives bring multiple categories to bear as they tell why their solution was effective, and we could not fit on the chart (Quinn and Rohrbaugh 1983) some criteria mentioned. This finding is understandable. Middle managers have a narrower task range than executives, so although we may use the same words to describe executive and middle manager activities in the decision-making process—identify problems, assess and prioritize alternative solutions, and then implement the preferred solution—the behaviors associated with mid-level and upper-level tasks differ.[5] By applying the Quinn and Rohrbaugh typology to evaluation statements made by middle and executive managers, the picture of a narrower task set for middle managers is painted in more detail. Quinn and Rohrbaugh (1983) have a reasonable indicator for managerial effectiveness, but it may be less appropriate for differentiating between managers operating at different levels of the hierarchy. Karl Weick (1978) argues that leadership effectiveness is measured best by the variety of ways the person can approach and conceptualize a problem. The variety of approaches these commissioners used to evaluate program success indicates their leadership ability.

Although managers and executives peppered their success stories with concrete evidence, the evaluation process, particularly for executives, included substantial subjectivity. The Quinn and Rohrbaugh (1983) typology allowed us to differentiate middle manager and executive thinking and behavior on evaluation. The typical middle manager employs fewer quadrants to evaluate the policy or program as a success, perhaps because middle manager tasks are narrower than executive tasks. The middles, nested within a confining decision-making structure, lack significant independent authority. Within their dense environment, achieving policy success involves working with, meeting, coordinating, and persuading others. Understandably, middles view their accomplishments as a joint effort and describe and evaluate their activities by using "we" rather than "I." The stories told by middles emphasize the skills that the literature on middle management competencies tends to emphasize: negotiating, persuading, and facilitating. In two stories where the middle manager has to fall back on the less-used skill of commanding, the manager expresses discomfort at having to confront a subordinate. A middle manager in F&A, after his commissioner supported him and rejected the budget proposal from the unit in mental health, spent considerable time with representatives from that agency to repair the damaged relationship (see chapter 5). Outsiders may consider command as being usual in the middle of the bureaucracy, but these effective middle managers rely primarily on their persuasiveness and decide or implement by command only as a last resort. Middle manager stories, in general, showed less complexity than executive stories and can be categorized more easily than executive stories.

Executives in a devolved organizational system live in a diverse, rich, policy world, with ultimate authority inside of the agency and access to influential individuals both inside and outside of government. Concerns for policy longevity and avoidance of negative publicity were expressed only by executives. Executives, not middle managers, were in a position to structure the policy in hopes that it could be maintained after their departure. Keeping their agencies away from negative publicity seeped into their discussions of evaluation. A good commissioner is not on the front pages of the newspaper.

Even when it appeared initially that they had lost, executives would not accept that outcome. They would try again, using another route if necessary, to accomplish their goals. Because of their location at the apex of the decision system, and because Alexander gave them carte blanche, they were in a position to be successful because they could define a substantial portion of their agenda. Middle managers were constrained by their structural location and the pressure of their ongoing, operational activities.

The Wallenda factor/executive hubris issue is important and constitutes a possible double bind for the cabinet member. The governor in a devolved system demands commissioner initiative and responsibility. This puts pressure on the cabinet member not to fail, more important personally because the issue may be self-selected. The cabinet member adopts the Wallenda posture of high confidence, which makes the cabinet member susceptible to hubris, which encourages overlooking or downplaying obstacles, thereby increasing the likelihood of failure. A leader who admits the possibility of failure risks diminishing the aura of power. The Wallenda factor, a presence in the executives' stories, creates a paradox of leadership—the requirement that the leader assess situations realistically in order to be successful, while also exhibiting optimism and confidence in a victorious outcome in order to motivate subordinates.

Middle managers and executives were conscious of evaluation. Middles were more focused on easily measured criteria than were the executives. Although the internal versus the external dimension of the middle managers' evaluation was clear, the issue of flexibility versus control was less clear. Flexibility dominated the success qualities demonstrated by these effective middle managers. They would adopt control strategies if necessary, but flexibility was the principal skill demonstrated in their stories. Executives easily moved around the Quinn and Rohrbaugh (1983) design, and beyond it. For executives, evaluation was more a management or leadership tool than a part of the decision-making process.

Having examined the complete policy-making model from both the middle manager and executive perspectives, in chapter 7 we will summarize our findings, discuss the implications, and recommend further research opportunities.

SEVEN

Conclusion

AGENDAS AND DECISIONS seeks to inform both theory and practice about how executives and middle managers in a devolved, state-level management system make and administer policy. Theory knowledge (knowing what) and practice knowledge (knowing how) are found in the authors' descriptions and analyses; practice knowledge is embedded in the descriptions, especially in each manager's story.

Governor Alexander's management system stands as a prototype of devolved, strong cabinet governance at the state level. Agencies were led by managers rather than by policy experts. Cabinet members and other administrative appointees who proved themselves capable were elevated to more complex agencies. Offering competent executives the freedom to act can be risky; the governor forfeits some control over the wider policy agenda and loses leverage to encourage interagency cooperation. By various measures the system was successful. Governor Alexander was viewed favorably by Tennesseans. Commissioners reciprocated the governor's trust and support with loyalty and high performance. They took reasonable risks and worked energetically. Although cabinet members did not authorize middle managers independent authority within their spheres of responsibility, middle managers indicated that they could speak their minds, felt good about what they were doing, and defined their work environment as team oriented (Cunningham and Olshfski 1985, ch. 2). The Alexander administration provides a model of state-level, devolved management that appears to have worked effectively.

This book is built on stories. Lists of leadership competencies, theories, and principles offer useful academic knowledge, but lists, theories, and principles do not guide the practitioner facing a challenging situation. Theory knowledge—the ability to explain a complex system by employing abstract concepts—and practice knowledge—the ability to resolve effectively a challenging management issue—are distinct, different domains. For practice knowledge, stories are one of a limited number of ways for learning to improve one's performance. Stories communicate tacit knowledge by telling how a competent manager responded to a unique situation (Polanyi 1966; Czarniawska 1999). Reading stories about competent managers tackling difficult problems can expand one's repertoire of responses. Reading and listening to stories, like watching the expert at work, is a way to learn by vicarious experience.

Self-reported stories of executives and middle managers making and administering policy reveal aspects of the decision process that would not have emerged had we used structured interviews, newspaper reports, meeting minutes, agency rules and laws, or other methods of discovery as our primary source of information. In reflecting on the findings from our research, we will commence with the decision model and the devolved decision system, then move to the concepts of density and paradox, the strengths and shortcomings of the system, and close with devolved responsibility, practice knowledge, and theory knowledge.

THE DECISION MODEL AND THE DEVOLVED DECISION SYSTEM

The rational decision model could not encompass the dynamic, fluid process present in the managers' stories (Weick 1978). Executives and middle managers did not conform to any linear, sequenced, equilibrium, or incremental pattern of decision making. However, the rational decision components of identifying the problem, assessing alternatives, deciding, implementing, and evaluating provided a helpful template and vocabulary for describing and comparing the actions of middle managers and executives. Managers "loop" and "craft" as they move back and forth among the stages of the model seeking an effective, implementable decision or implementation strategy.[1]

In some stories, expected stages of the decision model seemed to be missing. When Commissioner Donelson decided to offer the University of Tennessee's Knoxville campus increased state funding in exchange for more rigorous admission standards, his proposal was transformed into policy with apparently little discussion prior to decision or implementation.

The literature states that executive tasks and middle management tasks differ. That distinction is confirmed by our study: the higher the level, the broader the view. Middle managers in DHS were concerned that child abuse had occurred and acted to punish the employees who allowed that inappropriate activity to occur. Commissioner Puett certainly did not condone child abuse, but her primary concern was larger—the credibility of the agency, so that DHS could continue to work effectively in that county. The middle manager defines the problem from within a narrow job scope. In defining an issue, the effective executive will likely view a wider landscape than the middle manager.

The simple decision model with which we framed decisions appears useful to theorists, and at the outset it made sense to the authors, but practicing managers operate differently. No manager articulated a decision process; no manager appeared to follow a decision process model. Managers seem to sense and construct a situation holistically rather than conceptualize a decision as discrete parts (Weick 1995). "Garbage can" and "multiple streams" models offer insight and visual images, but Weick's (1995) sense-making approach is likely more useful for the practitioner—looking at the situation, constructing reality, and then communicating that reality to others. These leaders took an approach compatible with "positive inquiry" (Peterson and Seligman 2003)—being optimistic about a successful outcome, involving and encouraging their subordinates, continuously preaching a positive message, and building on small wins. Managers are quick thinkers. As new information unfolds or new stakeholders appear on the scene, they may reconstruct their understanding of the situation, creating a domino effect on other aspects of the decision. The decision process that commissioners followed, whether in the situations arriving unexpectedly that they could not avoid, or in the issues they chose to pursue, cannot be captured by the rational decision model. Attempting to convey what transpired over the course of a decision within the confines of an objective decision process model does not do justice to the complexity of these leaders' thinking and acting.

Agenda Setting and Problem Identification

The first step in the decision process is agenda setting/problem identification and is governed by *position, politics,* or *perspective.* The manager or executive is handed an issue to deal with, simply because that is the manager's or executive's *position.* It is in the job description. These "handoffs" can come from any direction—from a superior, a subordinate, or a peer, and handoffs happen more frequently to middle managers than to executives. Handoffs based upon one's position description are the main source for the middle manager's agenda. Executives could not escape tasks being handed to them, but these items did not dominate their agenda.

Politics generates agenda items more for executives than for middle managers. Executives receive requests for action from political officials, legislators, interest groups, and citizens. Middle managers were largely insulated from political officials and legislators but were contacted by organizations and groups in areas where they had administrative authority, for example, in health or safety inspections, once these tasks were assigned to them.

Perspective, the manager's ideas of what needs to be done in the agency, was an unexpected, major component of the executive's agenda. Half of the commissioners told stories about issues they brought with them to the agency, or that they "discovered" in the agency. These chosen or discovered situations meshed with their interests, skills, or previous experiences and were a personal choice (Simons: nonresponsiveness of the General Services agency; Akins: classification/compensation; Farris: inventory; McCullough: property management; Sansom: expedited construction on stalled projects; Olson: departmental reorganization; Donelson: higher education). Picking the issues one chooses to address (agenda setting) is an important and underrecognized aspect of decision making by state-level agency heads in a devolved decision system. This finding has implications for the theory and practice of executive management at the state level. In selecting commissioners, the governor who wishes to use a devolved management system should examine carefully the potential cabinet member's record of job successes as well as the area of a candidate's technical expertise. A manager's past experiences are a good indicator as to the choice of agenda items on the job. Middle managers are constrained by their dense environment and have less latitude than executives to focus their attention and resources.

Considering Alternatives, Deciding, and Implementing

In examining the stories told by managers and executives, looping and crafting activities made it difficult to separate the alternatives assessment stage of the process from decision-making activities. For executives, and particularly for middle managers who were involved in a situation of high density, the whir of meetings around the questions of defining, solving, and implementing made it hard to separate the decision phases. Getting stuck, then looping back and forth through the stages of the policy-making model, is common. The middle manager may lack resources (spraying insects), an important partner may be reticent to move forward (advertising contracts or mental health centers), and success may depend on a manager's informal relationships. The backstage activities of middle managers as they define, decide, and implement are facilitated by personal networks and negotiation skills.

Implementation is the expected duty of middle managers. In the traditional image of a government bureaucracy, an agency head will decide on an implementation plan, then pass the plan to a subordinate. A frontline administrator will execute the plan, overseen by a middle manager. Rarely did significant matters proceed so simply.

Middle managers live in a high-density environment, and this tight web influences their problem-solving activities. Environment and issue density determine the pace and ease with which assessing alternatives and deciding among options will proceed. Meetings and conversations dominate the middle manager decision process. Assessing alternatives and coming to a decision are intertwined, as the middle managers meet with stakeholders to seek common ground. This ongoing, iterative process involves numerous small decisions involving participants with differing concerns about the issue. Trying to separate proposing alternatives from deciding among them is futile. During these discussions, implementation looms large for the middle managers, since while they are not only the ones to participate in deciding on the plan, they are likely to be charged with implementing the decision, which follows the same complex dynamic as deciding on a solution.

Although middle managers may have the authority to implement a decision by fiat, this option was rarely selected in the stories. Middle managers seem to have concluded that dictating what is to be done rarely results in the most satisfactory outcome. Having sharpened their communication and negotiation skills through their decision-making practice, they continue to use these skills as the method of choice during implementation.

A surprising implementation finding was that executives often choose to become involved. Implementation is not a widely discussed executive activity, yet executives, at the apex of a devolved administrative structure, can act swiftly and decisively. In cases involving a short-term crisis (hiring freeze), modeling appropriate behavior for middle managers (avoiding excessive inventory), or attempting finality and closure on a highly publicized problem (child molestation case), commissioners handled implementation duties themselves. At times the direct implementation of a policy by the commissioner is the most efficient way to solve the problem, since the middle managers are spared the meetings necessary to craft the implementation strategy.

Another reason for executive implementation is that implementation by the middle manager would less likely result in acceptance of the decision as authoritative or legitimate. Commissioner action highlights the issue's importance and the commissioner's intensity toward it. Because their likely tenure is less than three years, and because momentum dissipates quickly, commissioners intending change in their organization must quickly set the tone and embark on their policy priorities.

Evaluation, Leadership, and the Wallenda Phenomenon

Because all managers participating in this study were selected because of their reputation for competence, and because we asked the managers to select the managerial situation that they narrated to us, we did not try to assess success or failure in management performance based upon the managers' stories. Using the Quinn and Rohrbaugh (1983) model, we sought to understand and explain the tacit assumptions that competent state managers bring to their decision-making task and to differentiate middle manager and executive thinking and behavior on evaluation. We found middle managers' stories less complex than executives' stories, and middle managers' stories fit the Quinn and Rohrbaugh dimensions of structure and focus more easily than executives' stories. Middle managers could usually articulate their accomplishments in objectively measurable terms, viewed their success as a joint effort, and used the word "we" when describing their success as it fit their need for help from others in negotiating an issue through a dense environment.

Executives evaluated their policy outcomes from multiple perspectives, but the Quinn and Rohrbaugh model could not handle the multiple dimensions and complex dynamics of executive evaluation. Avoiding controversy and bad publicity mattered to the executives, as did a concern for the placement of a new policy or program so that it would stabilize and endure beyond the tenure of the executive. Considering trade-offs among various aspects of a complex policy and using a small incident to leverage a broader agency goal were competencies demonstrated by executives. No middle manager mentioned anything involving such strategic complexity. This may be a function of level rather than managerial skill, but nevertheless these qualities do differentiate the behaviors of competent executives from competent middle managers.

Another behavior that only executives exhibited was that some flatly could not recall any situation in which they were not successful. Using the "I" word, executives generally described their successes as personal accomplishments, and they did not fail. The evaluation stage of the decision process was not used by them to assess a policy outcome objectively; it was a moment of triumph to celebrate the agency's successful performance. Evaluation was used to build their credibility and enhance their reputation for leadership and to motivate agency employees to continue their good work.

DENSITY

Environment density and issue density account for the speed with which a matter proceeds toward resolution. Environment density is determined by the number of structural constraints in the decision location. Does the issue fall solely within the purview of one unit within a single agency? How many agencies must agree? What is the level of stakeholder involvement? The more units or people that must acquiesce to a decision, the greater the environment density and the slower the program or policy progresses toward successful completion. Mid-level managers cannot decide unilaterally unless the problem is technical or within the domain of their authority. High density exists when the issue includes numerous clearances and multiple participants at their level or higher. Executives in a devolved system have low environment density within their agency, but when dealing outside of the agency, commissioners may face the same high density routinely encountered by middle managers.

A second aspect of density rests with the issue itself. Does the issue arouse conflicting emotional responses within the legislature, among organized interests, with the general public, or inside of the agency? With low-density issues, the assessment of alternatives is separate from the decision. If little conflict surrounds a low-density issue, then assessment proceeds until the middle manager decides what to do or faces a deadline. If substantial conflict is present in a low-density issue so that the issue cannot be resolved, a higher-ranking manager decides, or the issue is dropped. So in low-density cases the assessment of alternative solutions separates from the decision, and the process becomes visible. Broad and intense conflict creates high density for the manager attempting to resolve the issue.

A low-density issue can speed through the process; a high-density issue demands time and a manager's creative effort to achieve success. The concept of density as defined here has not been applied previously to the administrative process. Environment density and issue density offer insight into why issues move quickly or slowly through the bureaucracy.[2] Middle managers are customarily embedded in a dense environment—whether meeting with stakeholders to decide on a policy, deciding on an implementation strategy, or monitoring a program to ensure that it is working properly.

PARADOX

Paradox was not an idea or a theme when this project commenced, but paradox can account for many of the findings here that confirm or extend ideas about the theory and practice of leadership and management. An essence of paradox is multiple, conflicting truths; or statements that seem both true and false at the same time. Balancing between the extremes can sometimes be an effective practical resolution of the paradox.

Paradox: Analysis and Practice, Practitioners and Scholars

Analysts seek to understand the successes and failures of those in leadership positions. What personal, structural, or situational factors account for success or failure? These are the questions of scholars, not practitioners. For practitioners, failure is just a side step on the way to success. Skilled practitioners persist until something they achieve can be described as a success, and they either terminate their involvement at that point, continue pushing until they are satisfied, or quietly let the matter drop. Action and analysis proceed simultaneously for practicing managers, and initial failure does not stop their effort to achieve their goal.

Paradox: Evaluation

Certainly managers should and did evaluate. In their stories middle managers had close at hand empirical evidence to show that they handled their situations competently. The insects were sprayed at the right time in the life cycle; the details of the reclassification were completed so that employees were paid correctly and on time, turnaround times in the print shop had improved, dramatic savings of cost and time were achieved by computerizing the data input on welfare cases, and an orientation program for the agency dropped complaints to zero.

A few middle-level success stories did not cite usual performance criteria, for example, the highly qualified employee that had been let go for attitude issues who was hired and rehabilitated by a middle manager in the Department of Revenue, or the F&A middle manager who found an institution more accommodating during the next year regarding budget matters. Middle managers sometimes used personal subjective evaluation criteria to justify their success.

For executives, numbers can show success when a manager takes initiative and commences a new technical process, as Commissioner Simons demonstrated from changes in printing, auto leasing, and reimbursement, which sped up these processes, improving both efficiencies and satisfaction levels for their clients. Commissioner Farris could show success from his discussions with the federal highway administrator, which led to federal legislation granting Tennessee matching funds for its off-system bridges, thereby bringing new dollars to the state, and his policy on signing purchase orders, which reduced inventory expenditures.

But numbers cannot be cited in every successful decision. Commissioner Puett's decision on the child molestation case, when finally resolved, was accepted by all parties, and the issue never arose again. It was acknowledged as a success because the issue ended. Commissioner Donelson's decision to centralize rather than decentralize the computer function could not be established as a failure by numbers, but Donelson knew it was wrong. Darrell Akins could not show savings to the state for all of the work he did on revising the classification/compensation system, but there was agreement that the new system was a needed improvement. Akins could, however, show that increasing the longevity pay, a part of the total compensation package, was the least expensive way to satisfy the state employees association.

On some matters, the numbers speak loudly. On other matters, numbers are silent, and success or failure must be constructed in the hearts and minds of the observers. In some situations, quantification is appropriate, but not always. From a manager's perspective, the outcomes from some "right" decisions are obvious.

Resolving a problem so that the manager is happy or proud is an element of the evaluation process overlooked in the literature. But feelings of accomplishment and pride showed up as an important component of the discussion of the evaluation process. Evaluation is paradoxical—sometimes objective, empirical data are convincing; sometimes an objective standard cannot adequately measure success or failure.

Paradox: The Wallenda Factor

A paradox visible in leader stories here involves the Wallenda phenomenon—extreme confidence in one's actions which inspires followers to join and to exert themselves mightily in service to the agency, coupled with the reluctance to identify or accept failure in the course of doing the job. Commissioners in this book saw blips, minor setbacks and false starts, but not failure. A balanced appreciation of performance was absent from their statements to us. Perhaps leadership image is enhanced by the confidence among subordinates and the public that success breeds. And confidence motivates followers. Rational, unemotional analysis of strengths and shortcomings may engender doubt. For leaders and followers, evaluation means celebration. This is not to say that the executives did not rationally analyze their situation, but they avoided communicating shortcomings that may have been present in their analysis.

SYSTEM STRENGTHS

Devolution of responsibility is the regular mantra for organizations nowadays, and Governor Alexander devolved responsibility to his cabinet. Commissioners had unfettered power inside of their departments. Fiercely loyal to the governor, they also identified strongly with the perspective of their agencies. They did not act as hired guns of the governor, nor were they "stuck down" (captured by the bureaucracy), as F&A Commissioner Donelson suspected some commissioners might be. These commissioners seized the opportunity that Alexander offered, seeking ways that they could "make a difference," given the constraints of agency obligations, their personal background and expertise, and their views of agency needs. Commissioner Farris exploited his political connections to obtain federal support for highways and bridges in the state; Akins, helped by his personal connection with the F&A commissioner, reformed the state's classification/compensation system; Simons built General Services into an organization providing other state agencies with the tools they needed to do their jobs promptly, and at a lower cost. These projects were initiatives taken by commissioners, projects within their agency's jurisdiction that commissioners thought were priorities for improving the way of life for Tennesseans. These were more than projects and decisions; they were commissioners' passions about their jobs. They could not fail, and a momentary setback meant redoubled effort on the part of the commissioners, always exploring alternative paths to achieve their goals.

Commissioner enthusiasm infected some middle managers. Commissioners, by involving themselves down in the agency and showcasing a middle manager's successful project, set the informal norm that high performance is rewarded. The commissioner is committed to it, and those middle managers listening would be wise to respond enthusiastically and effectively if called upon, for the commissioner is paying attention to what is going on down in the bowels of the department. The commissioner celebrates a successful conclusion, praising those involved for their performance, hopefully motivating many to continue or commence high performance. What gets rewarded gets done, and public praise from the highest official in the agency is valuable currency. A devolved system can spark innovation and enthusiasm inside of an agency, as was shown in the automatic teller machines, which both saved money and sped up the response time to needy citizens.

SYSTEM SHORTCOMINGS

Commissioners had broad latitude and would protect their turf. Attempts to poach another agency's program for seemingly greater efficiency got nowhere, to the frustration of some middle level managers who envisioned synergies from cross-agency cooperation. During the latter part of the second term Alexander extended financial incentives for cooperative programs across agency lines. Although giving lip service to cooperation, these programs bore little fruit. Commissioners continued to protect their domains. Neither the F&A commissioner nor Alexander took the tough line to demand adherence to administration intent in the forceful way that Donelson had addressed budget issues at the beginning of the first administration. By the absence of follow-through, implicitly Alexander rewarded those who were reticent to cooperate.

The strength of a devolved government system lies in the high level of motivation among commissioners and the excitement that trickles down to middle managers who have close relationships with their commissioners. The weakness of a devolved administration emerges when programs require cross-agency cooperation, and commissioners drag their feet. A middle manager describes a situation from his perspective, where interagency cooperation was snuffed:

> We developed at the staff level a pretty good consensus around this case management model. The time came to consult the commissioners individually, and several of the commissioners bought off on the idea, one or two seemed ambivalent, and one reserved judgment. Commissioner Puett, who happened to be chairperson of the cabinet council, became a bit wary of this independent advisory body that really didn't have any real tie to any particular agency and had so many strong personalities. It really had very much a mind of its own, and so when the time finally came to make the presentation to the full cabinet council after we had lobbied, a signal was sent just before the meeting that Commissioner Puett felt that it was not the appropriate time to make the presentation, or at least to advance this particular idea, but she would entertain the presentation nonetheless.

> The chairperson and I, who had worked very closely developing this, said, "Well, let's go with the presentation, we're gonna have one or two advisory group members along with us to make this presentation." ... Two of the three advisory group members who were supposed to be at the group presentation couldn't make it for various and sundry reasons, and as it ended up, the chairperson and I were the two to make the presentation, and the burden fell on me to make the technical presentation. There's no experience like having a commissioner who is obviously put off with you standing in front of you telling you basically, "Look, now is not the time, I don't want to hear it." ... She did it quite diplomatically, but nonetheless expressed her views forcefully enough that one or two of the commissioners that we counted as votes got very quiet, and so I had this very uneasy feeling of twisting in the wind.

The governor could attempt to engender cooperation between agencies by financial incentives, but the implementation relied on those commissioners who may have been reluctant to share both responsibility and control. Minimal effort was exerted to curb the power of individual commissioners, or to demand cooperation. Devolving power to the cabinet was the foundation of the Alexander system, constituting both its strength and its weakness.

A DEVOLVED STATE MANAGEMENT SYSTEM: FINAL THOUGHTS

In a devolved management system responsibility rests with the cabinet member; so commissioners face pressure to perform competently. Much is made these days about the importance of devolved management and organizations, and devolvement is an important management tool, but no guarantee of success. If the superior does not trust the subordinate, and/or the subordinate fears that failed initiatives will be punished, then initiatives will not be forthcoming. Or, perhaps more dangerous to the organization, a subordinate who is ignored may take decisions and pursue initiatives that are contrary to the interests of the larger organization. Commissioners did not devolve the power of initiative to middle managers. However, competent commissioners consulted extensively with their subordinates, praising agency employees both privately and publicly, so assistant commissioners and directors felt included in agency decisions and respected by their executive.

Although we did not query commissioners about their reluctance to devolve responsibility, several reasons are possible. Commissioners generally do not know the value systems or work habits of subordinates, so the easy rapport that develops by years of working together, as can occur in the private sector or in middle levels of the public sector, was missing from the commissioner-subordinate relationship. Most managers, public or private, would be reluctant to devolve important tasks to people with whom they have not developed a trusting relationship. Moreover, the governor is elected, while commissioners are appointed. The buck stops with the governor. If a middle manager blunders not only is the commissioner at risk but the governor as well. A commissioner may be willing to take personal risk but not wish to jeopardize the governor for a middle manager's mistake.

It appears that motivating a middle manager to perform well is not so much a matter of devolved versus centralized structure between commissioner and middle manager but rather the presence of mutual respect and honest communication. Perhaps the effective leader/manager is one who maintains close personal contact, praising publicly while confronting privately, and who mentors the subordinate. To develop high morale in an agency, offering a middle manager responsibility and control may be less important than regularly demonstrating trust and respect through body language and actions as well as words, for talk may appear cheap these days.

Alexander's governance system, which devolved power and authority to the cabinet, unleashed energy and generated commitment at the commissioner level. Commissioners grabbed the opportunity and ran with it. They used various methods to achieve high performance within the agency: deciding and implementing personally, delegating tasks to subordinates while being supportive and holding subordinates accountable, and working closely with subordinates in generating and assessing alternative solutions. Both commissioners and middle managers approached their tasks pragmatically, neither hiding nor parading their values, while focusing on an outcome that would work.

The practice knowledge that one takes away from these stories cannot be summarized. Everyone will come away with a unique interpretation. People can only learn what they almost already know (Agnew and Brown 1982), and the stories of commissioners and middle managers offer opportunities for learning at all levels.

Our study of this state governance system supports theory knowledge arguing for the following:

- subjectivity rather than objectivity of administrative decision processes
- problem identification as the most important decision stage
- commissioner agenda setting as determining policy priority in a devolved system
- the importance of garbage cans/multiple streams and density in understanding the processing of issues
- sharp differences between executives and middle managers in the competencies demanded for effective management
- the paradoxical nature of leadership

Appendix

METHODOLOGY

While a quantitative research paradigm is superior for finding associations among variables in a large population, qualitative research works particularly well for learning how a total system operates (Diesing 1971). A qualitative approach attempts to explain parts and their interrelationships in a complex human system. The appendix summarizes the dispute between quantitative research and qualitative research, then describes how our project evolved from a quantitative emphasis during design and data gathering to a qualitative emphasis during analysis.

QUANTITATIVE VERSUS QUALITATIVE RESEARCH

Both quantitative research and qualitative research have strengths for the conduct of inquiry. *Quantitative* research gives priority to method over substance. Truth emerges from the *process*. Following standard rules of procedure in carrying out research will reduce the likelihood of error, and repeated testing furthers an ongoing search for truth. Content subordinates to method. *Qualitative* research emphasizes substance over method. Qualitative researchers pursue their subject matter by any method that will shed light on the topic; method subordinates to content.

Quantitative researchers do not object if a scholar pursues content over method, but the findings from qualitative research are considered at the "level of discovery," constituting speculation, not science (Falco 1973, 51; Kaplan 1964, 13–14). Speculations must undergo testing according to acceptable, scientific procedures before being admitted to the accepted body of contingent knowledge. Verifiability—stating propositions operationally so that prior studies can be replicated and the findings checked for consistency—is an essential criterion for acceptable quantitative research (Bergmann 1958, 24–28; Kaplan 1964, 38).

Qualitative researchers would respond that *all* scientific knowledge, whether called "quantitative" or "qualitative," is contingent truth, to be confirmed or adjusted in light of evidence (Gummesson 1991). A general statement, hypothesis, or theory is never finalized but transcended by subsequent research. Qualitative researchers employ quantitative findings as evidence, but they do not accord these findings priority status. Numbers can be revised up or down based upon information available to the researcher (Diesing 1971, 171).

Quantitative scholars insist on falsifiable hypotheses tested by carefully documented procedures that are subject to verification by succeeding researchers. Evidence not susceptible to retest under specific conditions is *unreliable* (Blalock and Blalock 1968, 12). Qualitative researchers throughout their project reinterpret their information as they gain additional evidence or insight. They would argue that *validity* emerges from the "creative use of bias" (Diesing 1971, 199). Diesing (1971) counsels the researcher to keep an open mind during data analysis. This advice is based on the assumption that bias cannot be eradicated. If one cannot get rid of bias, then use it wisely! Seek disconfirming evidence. In this project the stubbornness of each author ensured that the data were ransacked for countervailing information and alternative themes.

BUILDING THEORY FROM BELOW

"Grounded theory" (Glaser and Strauss 1967) describes our research. Grounded theory looks to create or test an empirical theory "bottom-up" by linking specific instances to larger ideas. Strauss and Corbin (1990, 21–22) offer three guides for qualitative research studies: (1) Let the informants speak for themselves. (2) Give an accurate description of the context. (3) Let theory emerge from the specifics. In *Agendas and Decisions* we describe the context, quote extensively from the subjects, and then link conclusions regarding manager/leader competences closely to the statements of those interviewed.

As we read and reread the interviews, the information seemed most tractable to social construction (Berger and Luckmann 1967). Each of us defines (constructs) reality. Two managers looking at the same situation may "see" different realities. Reality is not only objective, "out there," as the quantitative researcher would assume, but reality also is constructed in the head of each individual. The usefulness of this constructivist assumption is demonstrated by interviews with two commissioners from the Department of Personnel. Commissioner Darrell Akins saw the department as being too rigidly organized, for individual skills and task responsibilities did not mesh. To deal with this situation, he shuffled responsibilities to accord with the special skills of his managers, allowing each manager to take on tasks best fitting his or her abilities, in the process disregarding formal job descriptions. Martha Olsen, the next commissioner of personnel, saw the agency as lacking an understandable structure. She reorganized, making sure that job responsibilities meshed with job descriptions (rather than incumbent skills). What constituted a solution for Darrell Akins was seen by Martha Olsen as a problem requiring attention. Karl Weick (1995), following pioneers Berger and Luckmann (1967) and Bateson (1972) in the constructivist tradition, uses the word "sensemaking" to describe the process. Weick describes how managers and organizations participate in creating their own reality. "Sensemaking" has the paradoxical quality of simultaneously being influenced by reality and constructing one's own reality.

Quantitative researchers insist that each variable must be unambiguously defined. Open-ended, vague, or multiple definitions are not permitted. However, open-ended, vague, paradoxical situations are a reality that managers face every day. A qualitative design can handle complex and ambiguous situations more effectively than a quantitative design.

RESEARCH DESIGN

Both Olshfski and Cunningham were trained in the quantitative tradition, and quantitative processes dominated the research design phase. Choosing managers to be interviewed emphasized method over subjective judgment. Based on their management competence, state government middle managers were selected by a committee of commissioners and peers to attend the Tennessee Government Executive Institute (TGEI). Each attendee from 1984 to 1986 was interviewed by one of the authors, and their stories constitute our middle manager data set. These outstanding middle managers selected the ten best commissioners of the Alexander administrations. From a list of all commissioners who served between January 1979 and June 1985, each member of the TGEI class of 1985 marked by secret ballot the ten commissioners each middle manager thought most outstanding. The ten commissioners with the highest number of votes were interviewed. No commissioner selected refused to be interviewed; all ten commissioners were cooperative and forthcoming in their responses and generous with their time.

A qualitative research design might have triangulated the middle manager list of outstanding commissioners to ensure that viewpoints of informed individuals, such as journalists who follow state management, Alexander staffers who monitored various agencies, and stakeholder groups for the agencies, be included in determining the top ten commissioners. By listening to the reasons supplied by these knowledgeable people for selecting the top ten commissioners, a qualitative researcher would decide who to include in the group to be interviewed. For the qualitative researcher, the reasons for inclusion—the answers to the "why" question—are more important than checking off names to the "who" question. Aggregating the information supplied by knowledgeable persons provides a rationale with specific content—*why* the individual is an outstanding commissioner—information that would be important to the qualitative researcher. A qualitative researcher would likely criticize the commissioner selection process for failing to obtain the perspectives of knowledgeable people with diverse viewpoints.

Therefore, in selecting commissioners, procedure trumped content, which should please quantitative researchers but might be criticized by qualitative scholars. We also conducted long interviews with Alexander staff members and other close observers of the state political scene, thereby providing a validity check on the cabinet member interviews.

A second quantitative element in the research design involves the decision model. Our decision process model resembles other decision models, was set out in advance, structured the interviews with both middle managers and executives, and served as a checklist for probes. Managers were gently directed during the course of the interview to include information describing their activities according to the categories of the model. This is a quantitative approach: frame the model, and then collect information from all interviewees in order to compare responses for these categories (May 1994). This decision process model is set out in chapter 2.

The selection of commissioners and the interview schedule are compatible with a quantitative design. However, the interview and data analysis components of our research are qualitative, generally falling within the ethnographic tradition. Ethnography seeks to understand whole systems by studying the patterns of social interaction in a particular setting, attempting to uncover why people do what they do (Jones 1988) and learning from people rather than studying them (Argyris et al. 1985, ch. 6). Research information comes from the respondent's experience (Schein 1987). In the field the ethnographer uses multiple techniques to learn how managers make sense of their situations (Boghdan and Taylor 1975). Meaning is socially constructed and changes over time (Morse 1994). The good researcher is led but always in control (Banister et al. 1994). The common behaviors/attitudes (the culture) of some collective are central (Boyle 1994).

For the middle manager sample, our research also represents "action science," a process in which clients and researchers learn from each other (Argyris et al. 1985; Gummesson 1991, ch. 4). The middle managers taught us about state government; we, and other presenters at the executive development sessions, discussed with middle managers suggestions for improving the performance of their organizations. We worked with middle managers to understand their situation and to improve their effectiveness (Schmidt 1993).

This process resembles the appreciative inquiry approach to research and con-sulting. One approach to appreciative inquiry asks people to tell stories describing what they are doing when they are working at peak performance (Barge and Oliver 2003; Cooperrider and Whitney 1999; Srivastva et al. 1990). In dialogue with consultants and others in the organization, partici-pants explore, find, and implement ways to take their good personal and orga-nizational performance and make it better.

The four-stage decision process quantitative design was effective for mid-dle managers, but it did not flow smoothly for executives. Executive stories did not follow the stages of the decision model, even after probes. Some prob-lems were defined and then handed to a subordinate to solve; other situations, once defined by the commissioner, required no further managerial decisions for the solution and implementation stages. For the quantitative researcher, these data are missing, allowing the corrupting influence of bias to enter. The qualitative researcher, on the other hand, seeks to understand the decision processes underlying each situation and develop alternative decision models reflective of these situations. We did not abandon the model that served as the framework for our discussions with the executives. Rather, we expanded the scope of the inquiry in order to capture more stories and more examples of executive thinking as they moved through their convoluted decision processes.

STORIES AS DATA

Ethnographers rely on information derived from inside (emic) data and out-side (etic) data to describe and explain. Our principal evidence is emic data, the personal stories told by middle managers and executives recounting events in which they participated. Interviews with Alexander staff people, close observers of the Tennessee political scene, newspaper and journal accounts, two books written by Alexander (1986, 1988), and conversations with a num-ber of people whose paths crossed the events associated with the Alexander administration constitute etic data used in this research.

Stories construct an institutional history for the organization (Boje 1991) and capture life by bridging theory and practice in a way that facts cannot (Czarniawska 1999). Stories diagnose the organizational culture (McConkie and Boss 1994) and allow the deep structure to become visible (Dyer and Wilkins 1991), helping the listener understand the theories under which the teller is operating (Hummel 1991), or helping managers do their jobs better (Herzog and Claunch 1997). Story images communicate more accurately and effectively than numbers or didactic sentences. "Where practical choice and action are concerned, stories are better guides than rules or maxims . . . stories are the natural mediators between the specific and the general" (Robinson and Hawpe, in Vitz 1990, 711). Hummel (1991) cites Heidegger's statement that an approach must be adequate to the object. Understanding a manager's style and orientation to the job cannot be gained easily from a large, impersonal data set. Stories enlighten both practitioner and theorist.

The stories represent decision processes characteristic of upper and middle managers during the Alexander administration. Schein (1987) points out that upper-level managers are often inaccessible to ethnographers. We were fortunate in having access to middle managers who knew and trusted us because we worked with the TGEI management development program. This trust, developed with middle managers over several years, provided an entrée to the commissioners, who knew of us through their middle managers.

Commissioners who are prepared to tell their stories offer a rich data source. Here, competent cabinet members and competent middle level managers tell stories about decisions in which they were involved. The recounted events reveal the teller and the situation without divulging political secrets or rendering the narrator uncomfortable. A commissioner's story describes the person and the agency and connects the commissioner to other participants in the decision. Commissioner stories provide the broad context for middle managers' stories and substantial information about the management style of Governor Alexander.

Managers told of specific incidents—management situations—that were successful, where they performed well as managers. Commissioners want these stories to become foundation principles, or myths, for their agencies, because employees who have internalized the organization's stories know the commissioner's wishes for the agency and need less supervision (McConkie and Boss 1994). In their stories, Alexander's cabinet members often mention the governor, thereby communicating important insights about how Alexander related to his top administrators, as well as how these cabinet members related to peers and subordinates. Stories told by assistant commissioners and directors include in the narrative superiors, peers, subordinates, and clients, but they do not connect to the governor.

Can stories further knowledge? Can the stories be believed? Does one's perception, self-interest, or vanity distort reality? These questions raise several issues: (1) the universality of bias, (2) the purpose of the interviews, and (3) the priority of principles over facts.

UNIVERSALITY OF BIAS

Everyone has a unique perspective. Even though creating a research design to capture the same phenomenon, one person's physical location, fund of information, or life experiences will differ from another's, so whether the research instrument is an "objective" questionnaire or an open-ended interview, bias is present. Using a quantitative design does not remove the respondent's bias in selecting variables, definitions, and populations. The qualitative scholar assumes bias and then works through the bias, consciously reflecting with the reader on the ways that bias may be present in the reported research.

Purpose of the Interviews

For the scholar seeking to understand decision-making patterns in an organization, the key issue is not the substantive outcome—whether the manager was successful, or how successful—but the values and style embedded in the narrative. How does one relate to subordinates, peers, and the next higher level? How does this manager act in order to be effective within the system? These issues interest the scholar, issues to which the interviewee, even if desiring to slant the story, would unlikely be sensitive. Therefore, responsiveness bias by the respondent is unlikely to distort the interview story in a way that would corrupt the study.

Priority of Principles over Facts

The interview purpose is the principles that underlie the story. The story points beyond itself to management principles. Management principles are reflected in the practices described in the story (Mitroff and Kilmann 1976). These managerial principles and style emerge from the background information as well as the story content. A manager's style is rarely a matter of public concern, so there is no motive for dissimulation. Nor does one's managing style change easily. Individual behaviors develop slowly over a number of years. Michael Kirton (1989) argues that managing style reflects a personality factor that is extremely difficult to change. We believe that a manager's stories reveal truths about that manager's typical way of addressing situations, or style. Any tendency to exaggerate is counteracted by cross-reference through stories told by other respondents recounting the same events. "Making sense" (Weick 1995) is the appropriate criterion for checking validity.

In qualitative research, much is unanticipated, unexpected, and serendipitous (Jones 1988). Managers' stories resemble evidence gathered by participant observation, and participant observation is especially appropriate when the following are present:

- little is known about the phenomenon
- important characteristics distinguish insiders from outsiders
- the phenomenon is obscured from the view of outsiders
- the phenomenon is hidden from public view (Jorgensen 1989, ch. 1)

All of these attributes describe state-level governance.

Participant observation seeks themes rather than hypotheses, and attempts to gather information without disturbing the system (Schein 1987).

In manager stories as well as in participant observation, the researcher must select from the complex, ongoing reality those components that inform the research question. An interpretable whole emerges from constantly moving back and forth between facts and generalizations. The stories are windows into the lives of state government managers, with the time frame compressed to see the whole event.

Scholars indicate no one best way to lead or manage. Mintzberg (1987) speaks of management as craft, drawing an analogy between management and working with clay to form an art object. Effective managing—like painting, pottery making, music, and dance—involves creatively engaging a challenging task. Storytelling allows the researcher to witness the manager's creative moments. Past public manager stories have recounted the lives of tough, calculating, civic-minded heroes who walk at the edge of acceptability in order to achieve programmatic success, people such as Robert Moses, Hyman Rickover, and J. Edgar Hoover (Lewis 1980). This authoritarian style no longer claims universality. Scholars now celebrate the leader as facilitator or instigator, one who calmly negotiates the uncertain environment (Vaill 1989; Bennis 1999), or one who motivates a team to superlative commitment and performance (Quinn 1996). Others argue that effective leaders have a strong spiritual centeredness (Peck 1993; DePree 1992; Bolman and Deal 1995; Briskin 1996). Contemporary views on leading and managing show multiple effective styles. Qualitative research emphasizes the variation in a data set as well as modes and typicalities.

Audiotaping all interviews provided an exact record from which to recover the information. Because commissioners are used to having their statements a part of the public record, the presence of the tape recorder was comfortable for them. With middle managers, we had built credibility as academics who understood management and who both were knowledgeable about and sympathetic toward their work situations. Taped interviews reveal much more than the interviewers remember. Upon rereading the transcripts, new information emerges, and nuances appear that had been overlooked, allowing new interpretations grounded in hard evidence rather than in the researchers' faulty memories.

We believe the interview information has minimal distortion. A successful manager was telling a story he or she believed to be successful. There was no reason to dissimulate. Attempting to interview a political executive aggressively is likely to yield little useful information. Although commissioners are appointed by the governor rather than elected, all must respond to inquiries from legislators, citizens, and the media. They are experienced at avoiding issues they do not wish to address. If they are not reasonably competent at telling their stories in a way that is both true and protective of the governor, subordinates, and themselves, then they will not remain long in the cabinet. Any astute top manager wishing to keep information from an interviewer can do so. No academic interviewer can pry from an unwilling manager whatever secrets may be present. Academics are trained to understand and explain processes, not to uncover what is consciously hidden.[1]

The heavy use of direct quotations allows managers to speak for themselves and permits readers to draw their own conclusions from the data. Direct quotations assist such secondary analysis; accordingly, a substantial amount of directly quoted material is presented here. At the same time, a balance must be struck. Authors are obligated to select information that represents and clearly articulates the underlying themes so that the reader is not burdened with wading through reams of material (Boyle 1994).

DATA ANALYSIS

As mentioned earlier, we commenced with a quantitative approach, which bogged down the analysis stage. Commissioner interviews offered detail, but the information did not integrate well with our intended organizing structure. Our decision model did not reflect the way commissioners went about making decisions. We could have forced the data into the predefined decision stages and created categories for comparison, but we did not.

Qualitative research deals with wholes. Our collective whole is the upper level of the state governance system—governor, cabinet, and middle managers—during Lamar Alexander's tenure as governor. We seek to describe and explain the behaviors/attitudes associated with administrative decision making by Alexander's executives and middle managers during these eight years, from 1979 to 1987. "Grasping the native's point of view" Stewart (1998) and effectively integrating this point of view into the environmental frame is the analysis component of the ethnographic method. The validity of qualitative research findings is assessed by the plausibility of the whole (Atkinson 1990). Plausibility emerges from describing the environment and placing one's findings into this environment.

Stories convey truth in multiple ways. At a basic level, a contextually "thick description" (Geertz 1973, ch. 1) grips a reader's attention with the plotline. From an informational perspective, stories describe a particular situation, bridge theory and practice, and produce generalizations and insights without claiming universal status (Czarniawska 1999). To achieve understanding, one needs to know the actor's intentions, which is helped by knowing the setting. At an abstract level, principles can be distilled, which provide the basis for theoretical or moral precepts (Vitz 1990) and give people meaning in their lives (Mitroff and Kilmann 1976). Because each story involves a personal interpretation of events, the same story can be interpreted from a variety of perspectives. The ambiguities present in stories may frustrate those readers wedded to quantitative research; however, qualitative researchers see the richness of stories as conveying complex truths (Hummel 1991). The stories recounted herein provide "a social map to the uninitiated" (Wilkins 1984), an opportunity for the reader to enter vicariously into the world of the practicing manager. Stories bring a wide range of situations and allow various interpretations. There are no rules for guesses, but there are rules for validating guesses (Ricoeur, in Czarniawska 1999, 25). "Guesses" must mesh with other data to create a reasonable, interpretable whole.

After studying the stories to see how these Tennessee managers became aware of situations and identified problems, the thematic categories "position," "politics," and "perspective" emerged. Problems arrived on the manager's desk because whoever occupies the "position" (role) must address the situation. If you are the director of radiological health, then issues regarding X-ray machine safety come to you. The task may come from the commissioner above or from a subordinate below. You must deal with the problem because X-ray machine safety is within your job responsibilities. Second, "politics" is ever-present in public management. Pushed by various interests, issues with political implications come from every direction. Managers operate amid controversy. Any issue can become politicized. Last is the category of "perspective." Managers have their own unique issues that they wish to address. These personal agendas may not be part of the job description and constitute work above and beyond the challenges of position and politics. Perhaps the issue selected is an ideological passion, or perhaps the manager thinks that addressing this issue will make the department more effective. These issues are undertaken by choice, not by external mandate. The three themes of position, politics, and perspective organize the problem definition chapter. Our analysis is qualitative because the categories emerged from the data, and our generalizations remain close to the information from the stories.

In considering alternatives and coming to a decision, middle managers have a dominant style—meetings, meetings, meetings—while executives have a variety of styles—meetings for decision, meetings for subordinate input only, delegation, personal decision. Middle managers did not use the word "meeting" to describe their activities at this juncture in the decision process. They used words such as communicate, negotiate, convince, coordinate, gather input—but they did not say, "We met." Finally, grasping the context for these activities led us to the concept of density as a significant variable present in the middle manager's work life.

The interviews with middle managers conformed reasonably well to the decision-making frame posed at the outset: problem definition, alternatives and consequences considered before arriving at a decision, and then implementation. Evaluation with measurable indicators was common for middle managers. Executive stories meandered, with subplots and incidents tangential to the story line interweaving with each other, the narrative and commentary interspersed. Our promptings imposed some order, but not all steps of the decision process were described for each situation, nor were all steps important for each situation. Evaluation by commissioners rarely incorporated measurable indicators. They knew that an outcome was positive, or occasionally negative. Quantitative measures were not needed.

FROM A DEFICIT APPROACH
TO A POSITIVE APPROACH

Organization theory extant at the time we were observing and collecting stories did not provide a comfortable approach to analyzing our information. Scholars were parked in a "deficit approach" to the study of organizations: figure out what was wrong and develop a theory to fix it (Peterson and Seligman 2003). That was our starting point also. We discovered scholars who approach research differently: Karl Weick (1995) wrote about sensing situations rather than defining problems, and Peter Vaill (1998) advised (see Introduction) scholars to spend time researching exemplars rather than addressing problems. The rationale is that if you look for problems, you will always find some, regardless of how picayune the problems may be.

In 1990, Suresh Srivastva and David Cooperrider edited *Appreciative Management and Leadership*, which rejected the negative approach. In 1998, Martin Seligman, then president of the American Psychological Association, argued in his presidential address that psychology needed to make a positive turn to complement the deficit approach. Since the late 1990s, a number of collections and monographs have emerged championing positive organizational scholarship.[2] Mainline theorists in psychology and management have connected the dots among personality, organizational context, and culture to show that communication, affirmation, paradoxical thinking, and playfulness can create positive organizational change.

After starting with a deficit approach and a quantitative design, our analysis and presentation for *Agendas and Decisions* evolved into a qualitative approach and analysis. Stories, supplemented by interviews and available data, constitute the primary means for understanding Tennessee's state management system during the Alexander administration.

Notes

CHAPTER 1. INTRODUCTION

1. Beyle (1988) described Alexander and Matheson (Utah) as "two of the outstanding governors of the past decade." The Hartis (1985) article cites five public opinion polls conducted in Tennessee over the period 1979–1985. Alexander's "favorable" percentage ranges from a low of 68 percent to a high of 87 percent. For the positive opinions of state middle managers, see Cunningham and Olshfski (1985).

2. The U.S. military is adopting a similar process called "self-synchronization." "Self-synchronization requires headquarters to provide clear and consistent understandings of command intent, appropriate rules of engagement, and sufficient resources and then get out of the way unless asked for help" (Thompson 2006, 620).

CHAPTER 2. THE DECISION PROCESS MODEL, THE CULTURAL ENVIRONMENT, AND DENSITY

1. For a list of such models, see Zanetti and Cunningham (2000, 550).

2. Milward and Provan (1998) and Provan and Milward (1995) use the density concept to measure the connectedness among components of a system or network, specifically horizontal communications among service providers that share a common concern. Their concept refers to a known and stable group of stakeholders and agencies, and high density (communication among stakeholders and agencies) is seen as creating an effective system. As used in *Agendas and Decisions*, "density" is the number and intensity of stakeholders and agencies involved on a single policy issue. High density is neither desirable nor undesirable but simply characterizes the decision environment faced by the manager. Network theory emphasizes the structural aspects, the number and variety of administrative units not under one's authority (McGuire 2002); density as we define the concept also includes administrative units that may be under

one's authority but may oppose the proposal, political interests that have no administrative linkage to the issue, and the decision latitude permitted by one's superior. Networks on an issue will be easier to measure but may not capture the informal pressures with which the manager must deal. Our thanks to Ralph Brower for his insight on this issue.

3. The commissioner of personnel has the sole responsibility for developing and implementing the classification and pay grades for state government. Legislative action is not required to change or revise the classification plan and assign pay grades. Akins was lobbying the legislators for two reasons: (1) the Democratically controlled legislature would have to appropriate the money needed to fund the plan, and (2) if the Democrats or their constituency base thought the plan was poor or political, then they could sabotage the plan and also jeopardize other administration initiatives. The budget proposal for the year following the classification plan passed the House without concerns being raised about the plan.

4. "Satisficing" refers to a decision process which considers not every possible option, but only the array of options the decision maker considers reasonable; see Shafritz and Russell (2005, 53).

CHAPTER 3. PROBLEM IDENTIFICATION

1. "Problem definition" connotes an objectivist approach to knowledge. One studies a situation and seeks to uncover the problem that needs attention. "Agenda setting" fits more easily into a subjective approach. The manager selects an agenda among a variety of possible options, or chooses a particular definition from a range of ways that the problem can be defined. "Problem definition" is the term most commonly used and can fit either an objective or a subjective approach to reality.

2. Problems facing managers and executives can be divided into technical and managerial categories. Technical problems have a consensually agreed condition and an identifiable cause and effect. A technical problem involves something that was working, then stopped working. The problem would be solved by fixing it. There is no discussion of strategies for what needs to be done. The fixer accepts the original solution or plan and focuses on eliminating the problem. Technical problems have right and wrong solutions. Neither executives nor middle managers talked about technical problems. Managerial problems are called "wicked" (Mason and Mitroff 1981; Gortner 1991), "second order" (Argyris et al. 1985), or "third order" (Golembiewski 1979) because they lack agreed-upon definitions and solutions.

3. Viewing a problem in this way complicates the common method of defining organizational or managerial goals as a discrepancy between a desired state and the present situation (Schon 1983). One focuses top-down by using vision and goals or bottom-up by beginning with agendas and problems.

4. He and the commissioner of F&A were the only cabinet members to have frequent personal contact with the governor.

5. Donelson later served on the Tennessee Higher Education Commission.

CHAPTER 5. IMPLEMENTATION

1. Edelman (1964) emphasizes that legislation has both symbolic and tangible components. Embedded interests focus on the tangible aspects of policy, and these are spelled out in implementation, so interest groups will continue to lobby after the enactment of legislation. Often the subjects of that lobbying effort will be the implementing agency's managers.

2. The theory behind talking to achieve effective implementation is found in Fisher's and Ury's (1983) guide to negotiation, *Getting to Yes*.

3. Co-optation involves using one's power and influence to gain cooperation or accommodation. The classic study of co-optation can be found in Selznick (1949).

4. Brauer (1987) found that at the federal level political appointees averaged 2.2 years; Haas and Wright (1989) found among agency heads at the state level a 51 percent turnover every two years.

5. Akins had a close relationship with his middle managers. Not only did he know human resources theory and practice, which many personnel commissioners may not, he was a walk-around, hands-on manager who involved his team in departmental decisions.

CHAPTER 6. EVALUATION

1. "Means versus ends" categorizes the goal as intermediate or final. We found "means/ends" sometimes overlapping the "focus" dimension; at other times it was difficult to locate a decision on the "means/ends" dimension, particularly when the story involved interpersonal and morale issues. Therefore, we dropped this dimension.

2. We realize that one interview or one story gives an incomplete picture of a manager's competencies; nevertheless, even the blunt instrument of a single story shows consistently a greater variety of strategies, tactics, and outcome justifications used by executives than by middle managers.

3. Commissioner Steve Norris was not among our list of ten commissioners. He was not yet a commissioner when our survey was taken. A longtime state manager who worked his way up the ranks, as deputy commissioner of Employment Security Norris was credited with solving a severe financial problem in that agency and was expected to be named commissioner when the incumbent retired. Norris was passed over but soon afterward was named commissioner of the Department of Correction, tapped by the governor to lead an agency troubled throughout the Alexander administration. Norris was widely known and respected by middle managers throughout the state system and likely would have been selected among the top ten had his name been on the list when the survey was taken. In 2006, Norris was back in state government as deputy commissioner of the Department of Mental Health, serving under Governor Bredesen, a Democrat. The Tennessee health program, Tenncare had serious financial problems, and Norris was in the thick of attempting to create a financially solvent health care program.

4. Our initial interview plan involved asking commissioners for a failure story as well as a success story. We occasionally got a story of failure, but usually the multiple tales of success carried on long past one hour. Some commissioners could not recall a failure; others ignored the failure, or combined the failure with success by taking an initial failure and turning it into a success. The few admitted failures were smaller, technical issues that the commissioner subsequently corrected. As mentioned earlier, Commissioner Donelson initially refused to let agencies buy desktop computers, demanding that they centralize computing services with the state data services agency. When faced with evidence (or rebellion) by some agencies, he recanted and allowed the decentralization of information gathering and storage. He admitted that he had made a mistake in his decision to centralize the computing function.

5. The evidence from the interviews allows testing the theory that executives exhibit a broader managerial skill set than do middle managers. This test is powerful, because neither the interviewees nor we had in mind such a theory during the interview. Respondents were describing the situation they chose, prodded occasionally in order to ensure that all aspects of our decision model were touched upon. Biased responses induced by the interviewer or by an expectation that a certain type of answer would enhance their performance would not have been anticipated by the interviewee nor encouraged by the interviewer. The data constitute a measure with minimal bias.

CHAPTER 7. CONCLUSION

1. Drawing an analogy to his wife's working on a potter's wheel to craft a work of art from clay, Mintzberg (1987) uses the term *crafting* to describe what managers do as they work to create policy or solve a problem.

2. Note that an issue can be high conflict yet low density. The issue of budget for a mental health facility was high conflict yet low density and could be tracked by the model.

APPENDIX

1. However, if there is a widely understood and agreed counter-process that is not uncovered by the interviews, that is clearly in the domain of academic inquiry. *WASTA* (Cunningham and Sarayrah 1993) shows the societal pervasiveness of an unofficial decision process.

2. The *Handbook of Positive Psychology* (Snyder and Lopez), a tome of 829 pages, was published in 2002, followed by *Positive Organizational Scholarship* (Cameron et al.) in 2003. Representative of *Appreciative Inquiry* are Cooperrider and Avital (2004), Cooperrider and Whitney (1999), Fry et al. (2002), and Watkins and Mohr (2001). The academic center for appreciative inquiry is Case-Western Reserve University, and the Web site is http://www.appreciativeinquiry.cwru.edu. In the summer of 2006, Google showed more than one million hits for the term *appreciative inquiry*, which fits into the general field of positive organization scholarship (Cameron et al. 2003).

Bibliography

Adamany, David. 1989. "Successful Hands-Off Management." *Journal of State Government* 62:4: 140–46.

Agnew, N., and J. L. Brown. 1982. "From Skyhooks to Walking Sticks: On the Road to Nonrational Decision Making." *Organizational Dynamics* 11:2: 40–58.

Alexander, Lamar. 1986. *Steps along the Way.* Nashville, TN: Thomas Nelson.

Alexander, Lamar. 1988. *Six Months Off.* New York: Morrow.

Anderson, James. 2006. *Public Policymaking.* Boston: Houghton Mifflin.

Argyris, C., R. Putnam, and D. Smith. 1985. *Action Science.* San Francisco: Jossey-Bass.

Atkinson, P. 1990. *The Ethnographic Imagination.* London: Routledge.

Banister, Peter, Erica Burman, Ian Parker, Maye Taylor, and Carol Tindall. 1994. *Qualitative Methods in Psychology.* Buckingham, England: Open University Press.

Barge, Kevin, and Christine Oliver. 2003. "Working with Appreciation in Managerial Practice." *Academy of Management Review* 26:1: 124–42.

Barnard, Chester. 1968. *Functions of the Executive.* Cambridge, MA: Harvard University Press.

Barry, David, Catherine Cramton, and Stephen Carroll. 1997. "Navigating the Garbage Can: How Agendas Help Managers Cope with Job Realities." *Academy of Management Executive* 11:2: 26–42.

Bateson, G. 1972. *Steps to an Ecology of Mind.* San Francisco: Chandler.

Baumgartner, Frank, and Bryan Jones. 1993. *Agenda and Instability in American Politics.* Chicago: University of Chicago Press.

Bennis, Warren. 1999. "The End of Leadership." *Organizational Dynamics* 28:1: 71–80.

Bennis, Warren, and Bert Nanus. 1985. *Leaders: The Strategies for Taking Charge.* New York: Harper & Row.

Berger, Peter, and Thomas Luckmann. 1967. *The Social Construction of Reality.* New York: Penguin.

Bergmann, Gustav. 1958. *Philosophy of Science*. Madison: University of Wisconsin Press.

Beyle, Thad. 1988. "Governors' Perspectives" (book review). *Public Administration Review* 48: 664–66.

Blalock, Hubert, and Ann Blalock. 1968 *Methodology in Social Research*. New York: McGraw-Hill.

Boghdan, Robert, and Steven Taylor. 1975. *Introduction to Qualitative Research Methods*. New York: John Wiley.

Boje, D. 1991. "The Storytelling Organization: A Study of Story Performance in an Office-Supply Firm." *Administrative Science Quarterly* 36: 106–26.

Bolman, Lee, and Terence Deal. 1995. *Leading with Soul*. San Francisco: Jossey-Bass.

Bosso, Christopher. 1994. "The Contextual Bases of Problem Definition." In *The Politics of Problem Definition*, ed. David Rochefort and Roger Cobb, 182–203. Lawrence: University Press of Kansas.

Boyle, Joyceen. 1994. "Styles of Ethnography." In *Critical Issues in Qualitative Research Methods*, ed. Janice Morse, 159–85. Thousand Oaks, CA: Sage.

Brauer, Carl. 1987. "Tenure, Turnover, and Postgovernment Employment Trends of Presidential Appointees." In *The In-and-Outers*, ed. Calvin Mackenzie, 174–94. Baltimore, MD: Johns Hopkins University Press.

Briskin, Alan. 1996. *The Stirring of Soul in the Workplace*. San Francisco: Jossey-Bass.

Cameron, Kim, Jane Dutton, and Robert Quinn, eds. 2003. *Positive Organizational Scholarship*. San Francisco: Berrett-Koehler.

Cohen, M. D., J. March, and J. P. Olsen. 1972. "A Garbage Can Model of Organizational Choice." *Administrative Science Quarterly* 17:1: 1–25.

Collins, Jim. 2001. "Level 5 Leadership." *Harvard Business Review* (January) 79:1: 68–76.

Cooperrider, David, and Diana Whitney. 1999. *Appreciative Inquiry*. San Francisco: Berrett-Kohler.

Cooperrider, David, and Michel Avital, eds. 2004. *Constructive Discourse and Human Organization*. Amsterdam: Elsevier.

Cox, Raymond. 1991. "The Management Role of the Governor." In *Gubernatorial Leadership and State Policy*, ed. Erik Herzik and Brent Brown, 55–71. New York: Greenwood Press.

Cunningham, Robert. 1989. "Confront and Engage for Organizational Development." *Training and Development Journal* 43 (February): 71–72.

Cunningham, Robert, and Dorothy Olshfski. 1985. *Management Turnover in Tennessee Government*. Knoxville, TN: Bureau of Public Administration, UT-Knoxville.

Cunningham, Robert, Lori Riverstone, and Steve Roberts. 2005. "Scholars, Teachers, Practitioners, and Students: Learning by Fishing, Storytelling, and Appreciative Inquiry." *Journal of Public Affairs Education* 11:1: 45–52.

Cunningham, Robert, and Yasin Sarayrah. 1993. *WASTA: How Decisions Are Made in the Middle East*. Westport, CT: Praeger.

Czarniawska, Barbara. 1999. *Writing Management*. Oxford: Oxford University Press.

Denhardt, Robert, Janet Denhardt, and Maria Aristigueta. 2002. *Managing Human Behavior in Public & Nonprofit Organizations.* Thousand Oaks, CA: Sage.

DePree, Max. 1992. *Leadership Jazz.* New York: Doubleday.

Diesing, Paul. 1971. *Patterns of Discovery in the Social Sciences.* Chicago: Aldine Atherton.

Drucker, Peter. 2004. "What Makes an Effective Executive?" *Harvard Business Review* 82:6: 58–63.

Dunn, William N. 1981. *Public Policy Analysis.* Englewood Cliffs, NJ: Prentice Hall.

Durant, Robert. 1998. "Agenda Setting, the Third Wave, and the Administrative State." *Administration and Society* 30:3: 211–47.

Durning, D. 1987. "Change Masters for the States." *State Government* 60: 145–49.

Dyer, G., and A. Wilkins. 1991. "Better Stories, Not Better Constructs, to Generate Better Theory: A Rejoinder to Eisenhardt." *Academy of Management Review* 16:3: 613–19.

Edelman, Murray. 1964. *The Symbolic Uses of Politics.* Urbana: University of Illinois Press.

Falco, Maria. 1973 *Truth and Meaning in Political Science.* Columbus, OH: Charles Merrill.

Fisher, Joseph. 1989. "Helping the Governor to Manage." *Journal of State Government* 62:4: 131–35.

Fisher, Roger, and William Ury. 1983. *Getting to Yes.* New York: Penguin.

Fry, Ronald, Frank Barrett, Jane Seiling, and Diana Whitney, eds. 2002. *Appreciative Inquiry and Organizational Transformation: Reports from the Field.* Westport, CT: Quorum.

Geertz, Clifford. 1973. *The Interpretation of Culture.* New York: Basic Books.

Glaser, Barney, and Anselm Strauss. 1967. *The Discovery of Grounded Theory: Strategies for Qualitative Research.* Chicago: Aldine.

Glenn, T. 1985. "Executive Development: The Vital Shift." *Training and Development Journal* 5: 88–92.

Golembiewski, Robert. 1979. *Approaches to Planned Change, Part II.* New York: Marcel Dekker.

Gortner, Harold. 1991. *Ethics for Public Managers.* New York: Greenwood Press.

Granovetter, Mark. 1973. "The Strength of Weak Ties." *American Journal of Sociology* 78 (May): 1360–80.

Gummesson, E. 1991. *Qualitative Methods in Management Research.* Newbury Park, CA: Sage.

Haas, Peter, and Deil Wright. 1989. "Administrative Turnover in State Government." *Administration and Society* 21:2: 265–77.

Hartis, Nancy. 1985. "Alexander's Touch with the Public Awes Foes, Delights Friends." *Chattanooga Times,* August 26, p. A1.

Hayward, Mathew L., and Donald Hambrick. 1997. "Explaining the Premiums Paid for Large Acquisitions: Evidence of CEO Hubris." *Administrative Science Quarterly* 42: 103–27.

Herzog, Richard, and Ronald Claunch. 1997. "Stories Citizens Tell and How Administrators Use Types of Knowledge." *Public Administration Review* 57:5: 374–79.

Hirschhorn, Larry. 1988. *The Workplace Within*. Cambridge: MIT Press.

Hummel, Ralph. 1991. "Stories Managers Tell: Why They Are as Valid as Science." *Public Administration Review* 51: 31–41.

Jennings, M. Kent. 1998. "Political Trust and the Roots of Devolution." In *Trust and Governance*, ed. Erik Herzik and Brent Brown, 218–44. New York: Russell Sage Foundation.

Johnson, L., and A. Frohman. 1989. "Identifying and Closing the Gap in the Middle of Organizations." *Academy of Management Executive* 3: 107–14.

Jones, Bryan. 1994. *Reconceiving Decision Making in Democratic Politics*. Chicago: University of Chicago Press.

Jones, M. 1988. "Search of Meaning." In *Inside Organizations*, ed. M. Jones, M. Moore, and R. Snyder, 31–47. Newbury Park, CA: Sage.

Jorgensen, D. 1989. *Participant Observation*. Newbury Park, CA: Sage.

Kanter, Rosabeth. 1989. *When Giants Learn to Dance*. New York: Simon and Schuster.

Kanter, Rosabeth Moss. 1982. "The Middle Manager as Innovator." *Harvard Business Review* (July–August): 95–105.

Kaplan, Abraham. 1964. *The Conduct of Inquiry*. San Francisco: Chandler.

Kee, James. 1986. "Scott Matheson's Eight Principles for Gubernatorial Excellence." *State Government* 59:2: 64–69.

Kikoski, Catherine, and John Kikoski. 2004. *The Inquiring Organization*. Westport, CT: Praeger.

Kikoski, John. 1993. "Effective Communication in the Intranational Workplace: Models for Public Sector Managers and Theorists." *Public Administration Quarterly* 17:1: 84–95.

King, Cheryl, and Lisa Zanetti. 2005. *Transformational Public Service*. Armand, NY: M. E. Sharpe.

Kingdon, John. 1984. *Agendas, Alternatives, and Public Policies*. Boston: Little Brown.

Kirton, Michael. 1989. *Adaptors and Innovators*. London: Routledge.

Kohn, Alfie. 1993. "Why Incentive Plans Cannot Work." *Harvard Business Review* 71:5: 54–63.

Kouzes, J., and B. Posner. 1988. *The Leadership Challenge*. San Francisco: Jossey-Bass.

Kraut, A., P. Pedigo, D. McKenna, and M. Dunnette. 1989. "The Role of the Manager: What's Really Important in Different Management Jobs?" *Academy of Management Executive* 3:4: 286–93.

Lasswell, Harold. 1932/1960. *Psychopathology and Politics*. New York: Viking.

Lawrence, P., and J. Lorsch. 1967. *Organization and Environment*. Boston: Harvard Business School, Division of Research.

Lester, James, and Joseph Stewart. 2000. *Public Policy*. Belmont, CA: Wadsworth.

Lewis, E. 1980. *Public Entrepreneurship*. Bloomington: Indiana University Press.

Ludema, James. 2002. "Appreciative Storytelling: A Narrative Approach to Organization Development and Change." In *Appreciative Inquiry and Organizational*

Transformation: Reports from the Field, ed. Ronald Fry, Frank Barrett, Jane Seiling, and Diana Whitney, 239–61. Westport, CT: Quorum.

Lyles, M. 1981. "Formulating Strategic Problems: Empirical Analysis and Model Development." *Strategic Management Journal* 2: 61–75.

Maas, Peter. 1983. *Marie*. New York: Random House.

March, J. 1989. *Decisions and Organizations*. Oxford: Blackwell.

Mason, R., and I. Mitroff. 1981. *Challenging Strategic Planning Assumptions*. New York: John Wiley.

Matheson, Scott, with James Kee. 1986. *Out of Balance*. Salt Lake City, UT: Gibbs M. Smith.

May, Katharyn. 1994. "Abstract Knowing: The Case for Magic in Method." In *Critical Issues in Qualitative Research Methods*, ed. Janice Morse, 10–21. Thousand Oaks, CA: Sage.

McConkie, M., and W. Boss. 1994. "Using Stories as an Aid to Consultation." *Public Administration Quarterly* 17:4: 377–95.

McGuire, Michael. 2002. "Managing Networks: Propositions on What Managers Do and Why They Do It." *Public Administration Review* 62:5: 598–609.

Miles, Mathew, and Michael Huberman. 1984. *Qualitative Data Analysis*. Beverly Hills, CA: Sage.

Milward, H. B., and K. G. Provan. 1998. "Principles for Controlling Agents: The Political Economy of Network Structure." *Journal of Public Administration Research and Theory* 8:2: 203–21.

Mintzberg, H. 1987. "Crafting Strategy." *Harvard Business Review* 65 (July–August): 66–75.

Mintzberg, Henry. 1973. *The Nature of Managerial Work*. New York: Harper & Row.

Mitroff, I. 1998. *Smart Thinking for Crazy Times: The Art of Solving the Right Problem*. San Francisco: Berrett-Koehler.

Mitroff, I., and R. Kilmann. 1976. "On Organization Stories: An Approach to the Design and Analysis of Organizations through Myths and Stories." In *The Management of Organization Design*, vol. 1, ed. R. Kilmann, L. Pondy, and D. Slevin, 189–207. New York: North Holland.

Morse, Janice, ed. 1994. *Critical Issues in Qualitative Research Methods*. Thousand Oaks, CA: Sage.

Palmer, Parker. 1994. "Leading from Within." In *Spirit at Work: Discovering the Spirituality in Leadership*, ed. Jay Conger et al., 19–40. San Francisco: Jossey-Bass.

Parkhe, Arvind. 1993. "'Messy' Research, Methodological Predispositions, and Theory Development in International Joint Ventures." *Academy of Management Review* 18:2: 227–68.

Palumbo, Dennis, and D. Calista, eds. 1990. *Implementation and the Policy Process: Opening Up the Black Box*. Westport, CT: Greenwood Press.

Peck, M. Scott. 1993. *A World Waiting To Be Born*. New York: Bantam.

Peters, Tom, and Robert Waterman. 1982. *In Search of Excellence*. New York: Harper & Row.

Peterson, Christopher, and Martin Seligman. 2003. "Positive Organizational Studies: Lessons from Positive Psychology." In *Positive Organizational Scholarship*, ed. Kim Cameron, Jane Dutton, and Robert Quinn, 14–27. San Francisco: Berrett-Koehler.

Polanyi, Michael. 1966. *The Tacit Dimension*. Garden City, NY: Doubleday.

Polkinghorne, Donald. 1988. *Narrative Knowing and the Human Sciences*. Albany: State University of New York Press.

Pressman, Jeffrey, and Aaron Wildavsky. 1984. *Implementation*. Berkeley: University of California Press.

Provan, K. G., and H. B. Milward. 1995. "A Preliminary Theory of Network Effectiveness: A Comparative Study of Four Community Mental Health Systems." *Administrative Science Quarterly* 40:1: 1–33.

Quinn, Robert. 1988. *Beyond Rational Management: Mastering the Paradoxes and Competing Demands of High Performance*. San Francisco: Jossey-Bass.

Quinn, Robert. 1996. *Deep Change: Discovering the Leader Within*. San Francisco: Jossey-Bass.

Quinn, Robert, and John Rohrbaugh. 1983. "A Spatial Model of Effectiveness Criteria: Toward a Competing Values Approach to Organizational Analysis." *Management Science* 29(3): 363–77.

Raiffa, Howard. 1968. *Decision Analysis*. Reading, MA: Addison Wesley.

Reed, M. 1991. "Organizations and Rationality: The Odd Couple." *Journal of Management Studies* 28: 559–67.

Riveland, Chase. 1989. "Gubernatorial Styles: Is There a Right One?" *Journal of State Government* 62:4: 136–39.

Roberts, Deborah. 1986. "Governors and Top State Bureaucrats: Politics, Merit, or Hybrid?" Paper presented at the ASPA annual meeting, Anaheim, CA.

Rochefort, David, and Roger Cobb. 1994. *The Politics of Problem Definition*. Lawrence: University Press of Kansas.

Rokeach, Milton. 1970. *Beliefs, Attitudes, and Values*. San Francisco: Jossey-Bass.

Rosenau, Pauline. 1992. *Post-Modernism and the Social Sciences*. Princeton, NJ: Princeton University Press.

Russo, E., and P. Schoemaker. 1989. *Decision Traps*. New York: Simon and Schuster.

Ryan, Kathleen, and Daniel Oestreich. 1998. *Driving Fear Out of the Workplace*. San Francisco: Jossey-Bass.

Sabatier, Paul, ed. 1999. *Theories of the Policy Process*. Boulder, CO: Westview.

Sandelands, Lloyd. 1990. "What Is So Practical about Theory? Lewin Revisited." *Journal for the Theory of Social Behavior* 20:3: 235–62.

Schattschneider, E. E. 1960. *The Semi-Sovereign People*. New York: Holt, Rinehart, and Winston.

Schein, E. 1987. *The Clinical Perspective in Fieldwork*. Newbury Park, CA: Sage.

Schmidt, M. 1993. "Grout: Alternative Kinds of Knowledge and Why They Are Ignored." *Public Administration Review* 53:6: 525–30.

Schon, Donald. 1983. *The Reflective Practitioner*. New York: Basic Books.

Scott, William. 1979. "Leadership: A Functional Analysis." In *Crosscurrents in Leadership*, ed. J. Hunt and L. Larson, 84–93. Carbondale: SIU Press.

Selznick, Philip. 1949. *TVA and the Grass Roots: A Study in the Sociology of Formal Organization*. Berkeley: University of California Press.

Shafritz, Jay, and E. W. Russell. 2005. *Introducing Public Administration*, Fourth Edition. New York: Pearson Longman.

Snyder, C. R., and Shane Lopez, eds. 2002. *Handbook of Positive Psychology*. New York: Oxford University Press.

Srivastava, Sanjay, Knut Hagtvet, and Arun Sen. 1994. "A Study of Role Stress and Job Anxiety among Three Groups of Employees in a Private Sector Organization." *Social Science International* 10:1–2: 25–30.

Srivastva, Suresh, David Cooperrider et al. 1990. *Appreciative Management and Leadership: The Power of Positive Thought and Action in Organizations*. San Francisco: Jossey-Bass.

Stewart, Alex. 1998. *The Ethnographer's Method*. Thousand Oaks, CA: Sage.

Stone, Deborah. 1988. *Policy Paradox and Political Reason*. Glencoe, IL: Scott, Foresman.

Strauss, Anselm, and Juliet Corbin. 1990. *Basics of Qualitative Research*. Newbury Park, CA: Sage.

Thompson, Fred. 2006. "'Netcentric' Organizations." *Public Administration Review* 66:4: 619–22.

Vaill, Peter. 1989. *Managing as a Performing Art*. San Francisco: Jossey-Bass.

Vaill, Peter. 1998. *Spirited Leading and Learning*. San Francisco: Jossey-Bass.

Vitz, P. 1990. "The Use of Stories in Moral Development." *American Psychologist* 45:6: 709–20.

Watkins, Jane M., and Bernard Mohr. 2001. *Appreciative Inquiry*. San Francisco: Jossey-Bass/Pfeiffer.

Weick, Karl. 1978. "The Spines of Leaders." In *Leadership: Where Else Can We Go?*, ed. M. McCall and M. Lombardo, 37–61. Durham, NC: Duke University Press.

Weick, Karl. 1979/1969. *The Social Psychology of Organizing*. Reading, MA: Addison Wesley.

Weick, Karl. 1993. "The Collapse of Sense Making in Organizations: The Mann Gulch Incident." *Administrative Science Quarterly* 38: 628–52.

Weick, Karl. 1995. *Sensemaking in Organizations*. Thousand Oaks, CA: Sage.

Weimer, D. 1993. "The Current State of Design Craft: Borrowing, Tinkering, and Problem Solving." *Public Administration Review* 53:2: 110–20.

Weinberg, Martha. 1976. *Managing the State*. Cambridge: MIT Press.

Weissert, Carol. 2001. "Reluctant Partners: The Role of Preferences, Incentives, and Monitoring in Program Compliance." *Journal of Public Administration Research and Theory* 11:4: 435–53.

Whetten, David, and Kim Cameron. 1984. *Developing Management Skills*. Glenview, IL: Scott Foresman and Company.

Wilkins, A. 1984. "The Creation of Company Cultures: The Role of Stories and Human Resource Systems." *Human Resources Management* 23:1: 41–60.

Wrapp, Edward. 1967. "Good Managers Don't Make Policy Decisions." *Harvard Business Review* 45:5: 91–99.

Zahariadis, Nikolaos. 1999. "Ambiguity, Time, and Multiple Streams." In *Theories of the Policy Process*, ed. Paul Sabatier, 73–93. Boulder, CO: Westview.

Zalesnik, Abraham. 1991. "Leading and Managing: Understanding the Difference." In *Organizations on the Couch*, ed. Kets de Vries, Manfred et al., 97–119. San Francisco: Jossey-Bass.

Zanetti, Lisa, and Robert Cunningham. 2000. "Perspectives on Public-Sector Strategic Management." In *Handbook of Strategic Management*, ed. Jack Rabin, Gerald Miller, and Bartley Hildreth, 545–60. New York: Marcel Dekker.

Index